MENTAL
EQUITATION

A GUIDE TO INTERDISCIPLINARY HORSEMANSHIP

MENTAL EQUITATION

A GUIDE TO INTERDISCIPLINARY HORSEMANSHIP

JAMES R. ARRIGON

Alpine
PUBLICATIONS
Loveland, Colorado

Library of Congress Cataloging in Publication Data
Arrigon, James R., 1960-
Mental Equitation : a guide to interdisciplinary horsemanship /
James R. Arrigon
p.   cm.
Includes bibliographical reference (p.   ) and index.
ISBN 1-57779-010-3
1. Horsemanship.   2. Horses—training.   3. Horses—behavior.
4. Human-animal communication   I. Title
SF309.A66   1999   98-47580
798.2—dc21   CIP

This book is available at special quantity discounts
for breeders and for club promotions, premiums, or
educational use. Write for details.

1 2 3 4 5 6 7 8 9 0

Printed in the United States of America.

Editing: Erin McKay
Illustrations by N. J. Robinson unless otherwise credited
Photos by Jim or Gwen Arrigon unless otherwise credited
Design and Layout: Rudy J. Ramos, Ramos Design Studio
Front cover main photo (also on page 1) by A. Kumekawa
Back cover photo: Suzanne Ellenberger on Big Trouble
and Hallie Arrigon on Royce ride in front of MacCracken Hall
on the Miami University campus.

To my family,
Including all the furry ones.

CONTENTS

FOREWORD

When Jim asked me to write the Foreword for his *Mental Equitation* book, I spent some time with the manuscript. Immediately, I found myself relating Jim's methods to the ones I was taught as a young rider by Wayne Carroll and Victor Hugo-Vidal. Each chapter stirred memories of my own development as a rider, horseman, and person. More important than riding skills, Jim's mental equitation system helps you develop sound, basic skills that will serve you in life. Jim teaches discipline, hard work, and the pursuit of excellence in every area of your life.

Hail to the horse! Renowned for remarkable memory, loyalty, and eagerness to obey, horses have been helpful companions to man for thousands of years. For centuries, good horsemen have communicated with horses through fundamental natural aids. The effectiveness of that communication depends on the skills of the horseman. While each riding discipline requires a specific style, effective riding in *any* discipline demands strength, skill, and the ability to overcome and eliminate stress.

If the baseball player Jim mentions in Chapter 1 were a riding instructor, he would likely base his evaluation of mental equitation on the blue ribbons and trophies in the Miami University barn. Having personally visited the Miami campus on many occasions and observed Jim with his students, I know that Jim's enthusiasm, talent, and dedication to riding and teaching have been an inspiration to many former college riders who continue to enjoy their passion as adults, including several who now work professionally in the horse industry.

ROBERT E. CACCHIONE
Executive Director and Founder

Intercollegiate Horse Show Association
Fairfield, Connecticut

 CHAPTER ONE

MENTAL EQUITATION: AN INTERDISCIPLINARY APPROACH TO RIDING

I believe that all riding is interdisciplinary in nature, based on classical horsemanship that was established centuries ago. All the disciplines—Western, hunt seat, saddle seat, and so on—employ the same set of rules; they just use them differently to achieve their respective goals. As a college riding instructor with a plentiful supply of students, I often borrow from one discipline to make a point in another. For example, I've used reining techniques to teach jumping lessons and dressage concepts to teach hunter equitation. My Western riders learn to do two-point, post, and ride two-handed. I've even taught flying lead changes to reiners riding jumping horses!

WHAT IS MENTAL EQUITATION?

This book is about "mental equitation," a method for developing the common-sense, well-rounded, problem-solving ability that will make you a better rider—no matter what saddle you use! This method is based on the philosophy that riders can improve their effectiveness by using their minds as much as they use their bodies. While equitation stresses communicating with the horse using body position and cues, *mental* equitation stresses understanding why position and cues have a certain effect on the horse. I never teach riders *what* to do without making sure they understand *why* it must be done.

Mental equitation is a dynamic and reciprocal communication system in which the horse is trained to respond to the rider while the rider simultaneously responds to reactions from the horse. It's a practical approach to horsemanship that builds a rider *and a horse* from the ground up, one skill at a time. It involves recognizing your potential and figuring out how to reach it. And it's an approach that can be used with almost any discipline.

1

WHAT MENTAL EQUITATION
CAN DO FOR YOU

Mental equitation gives a rider the knowledge needed to communicate effectively with the horse. As an approach to riding, mental equitation focuses on the horse's intelligence and memory, his learning processes, and the instincts that affect his perception of the world and his training. Mental equitation provides an understanding of how riders and horses communicate, removing the uncertainties that create stress and replacing them with confidence.

Mental equitation improves a rider's sense of timing—the ability to respond appropriately to every situation. You've probably known someone who can get on the craziest, most out-of-control horse and *instantly* make a marked difference in that horse's behavior. Such a rider has great timing. Good timing involves a constantly changing flow of information from rider to horse and back again—cues and responses and counter-responses. Some people naturally have great timing, while other people develop a sense of timing through study and practice. The more educated and experienced you become, the better your timing will be.

One of my all-time favorite baseball players taught what I would call "mental hitting." He was fond of saying that "concentration is the ability to not think about anything." He said that when the pitch was coming, all you can do is clear your head and let your body and your senses take over,

reacting as you have prepared them to do. This philosophy, which is really about timing, applies to advanced horsemanship, as well.

In developing my mental equitation system, I studied how horses behave and learn, how horses and riders communicate, and how trainers can actually manipulate a horse's balance and movement. Since mental equitation requires an appreciation of all the ways in which a horse relates to the world around him, it is an ongoing process that is as much for teachers as it is for riders.

This book is not a comprehensive equitation or training manual; volumes have already been published about horsemanship and aids. Instead, this is a guidebook, a sort of map to help you navigate toward your goal of achieving your maximum potential as a rider. Many of my teaching philosophies (and philosophies for living) were developed while playing youth and high school baseball under the best coach I ever had—my Dad. He would tell his players, "I will never criticize anyone for being too slow, too small, or not having the skills to make a play. But there is never an excuse for not being smart enough!"

I am convinced that mental equitation makes smart riders and horses, and wins horse shows. Contrary to what some people think, the best teachers and trainers have no secrets. Their methodology is simple. What makes them champions is time well spent, attention to detail, hard work, a good plan—and the confidence and composure to carry it out. These are the things that bring success in any field!

"Mental Equitation" is making sure that you do things for a reason, because it makes sense to you. Take time to think about what you're doing on a horse. The answer to your training may be something seemingly unrelated. Most of all, don't follow the trends without thinking for yourself. By James Arrigon.

 CHAPTER TWO

UNDERSTANDING AND INFLUENCING HORSE BEHAVIOR

To understand mental equitation, let's start at the beginning, with a simple concept: horses are animals, not equipment or machines. That's obvious, right? Not necessarily. Many riders have the mistaken notion that riding is a cookbook sport—that if you take each step in order, everything works the way it should. I wish it were that easy.

Riding is different from most other sports because besides learning the physical aspect of it, you have to deal with the personality of your partner (the horse). In sailing, if you know your craft and execute well, you can pretty well expect the desired results. In riding, you can do *your* part perfectly and still not get the job done if the horse doesn't choose to do *his* job.

To use another analogy, riding is somewhat like basketball, where you can execute perfectly and still fail because of the people around you. I could make the greatest between-the-legs, looking-the-other-way pass in the history of basketball, but if it thunks off my teammate's forehead and out of bounds, I still look bad. It's the same way with riding horses.

UNDERSTANDING THE HORSE'S NATURAL INSTINCTS

As with most animals, horses exhibit instinctive behavior that developed over millions of years. Although a few major universities have conducted equine behavioral research (e.g., Montana State University, Texas A&M University, Colorado State University, and my alma mater—The University of Kentucky), not much scientific data is available in this field. Much of what we know about horse behavior and learning is passed down from

Horses are "gregarious" in nature, preferring to hang out in groups rather than going it alone.

Horses are "socially ordered," which means that some are dominant and others are subservient. Within a herd, every horse knows exactly which is tougher than which, and most fights occur when one of them tests the pecking order.

one generation to the next, in the barns and on the farms of the horse industry. If you have the time and patience to watch, you can learn about most horse behaviors firsthand.

Horses Are Gregarious

Undoubtedly, you've noticed that horses prefer to band together in groups than to be alone. A pack of weanlings or yearlings running shoulder to shoulder through the field is a common sight on breeding farms. I've learned to be alarmed when a horse is widely separated from the herd; such behavior often means he's sick or hurt.

A horse's gregarious nature can be a nuisance when you are trying to ride or get some training done and the only thing on his mind is getting

back to his friends. It's downright embarrassing when you are in the center of the show ring trying to do an individual test, and you can feel the horse drifting uncontrollably toward the group of waiting horses. And how often have you seen a perfectly good horse become an obsessed maniac when his stablemate leaves the barn?

Part of mental equitation is being smart enough to put your horse in situations that will be most to your advantage. For example, I try to ride horses I'm training when there are lesson groups riding also—*not* when everyone else is heading back to the barn. I also try to keep a very dominant horse apart from the others in a riding group so he won't be tempted to take a kick at another horse. To create successful, confidence-building experiences for your horse and yourself, you've got to ride smart.

Sometimes you can use a horse's gregariousness to your advantage. If a horse gets loose, where will he go? Through the gate and down the road? Probably not. Usually, a horse in a tense or unfamiliar situation will head for another horse. Even if he gets out in the middle of the night, you will likely find him the next morning standing face to face with a horse in a stall or on the other side of a fence. Or he'll be grazing nearby. You very rarely hear of a horse running away from the farm if other horses are there.

Horses Are Socially Ordered

Horse herds have a social hierarchy. Within their group, they will establish a fairly well-defined pecking order, with each animal dominant over certain others and subservient to the rest.

The best way to determine order of dominance is to watch a group of horses during feeding time. Once during a spring break here at Miami University, I fed horses in a pasture feeding line, with feed buckets tied to every other fence post. As I started dropping feed into a bucket at one end of the line, the most dominant horse in the group moved to it. When I filled the second bucket, the next most dominant horse stepped forward, and so on. I quickly learned the pecking order and found that it was remarkably consistent day after day.

Often, clashes occur while horses are trying to find their place in their group's social hierarchy. A new horse in a group confronts others to learn exactly where he fits. Sometimes it seems as though the new horse gets picked on when he's turned out with strangers, but he is not exactly being harassed. The others are testing him, and the discord will end soon. Quite often the horses that "picked on" the new horse at first will end up being subservient to him in the long run.

Many trainers feel that horses try to determine where humans fit within the hierarchy. You've probably noticed that your horse acts differently when someone else rides him. When a good horse is being stubborn or "mean" to a new rider, he could actually be trying to determine dominance or subservience. A good rider knows the importance of establishing dominance over each horse. You don't want to be mean or unreasonable, but everyone needs to be clear about who's in charge!

Horses React by Fight or Flight

Animals in the wild protect themselves in one of two ways: through fight or flight. Although the horse has a powerful and potentially destructive kick, he is much more predisposed to flee when frightened. This behavior presents itself as "spooking" or "bolting" and can be traced directly to his survival instinct. Back before horses were domesticated, they needed some advance warning in order for flight to be an effective means of protection, and so the species evolved with remarkably keen hearing, smell, and even touch.

Horses Have Limited Vision

Compared to other animal species, horses have fairly poor vision. In the early evolution of the horse, Eohippus lived in the underbrush of the swamp, where seeing predators would have been difficult even with keen vision. Through the process of natural selection, the horse's senses of hearing and smell became much more highly developed than his sense of sight.

Because his eyes are located on the sides of his head, a horse has largely monocular vision. He sees objects with one eye or the other, but

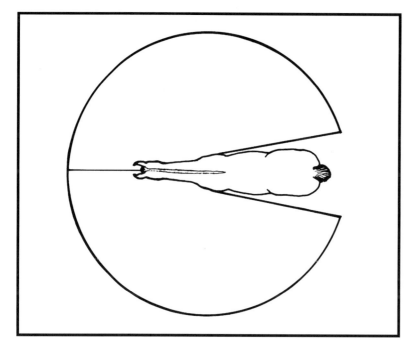

The horse has eyes on the sides of his head, giving him better peripheral vision than humans have. However, because his body is wider than his head, he can't see directly behind himself. When approaching from behind, it's important to speak to the horse to let him know you are there.

seldom with both. Therefore, he sees mostly in a two-dimensional field, with very limited depth perception as compared to a species whose eyes are located at the front of the face, such as with a dog or a human. (Think about *that* the next time you're galloping toward that tricky combination jump!)

A horse focuses most easily by looking down his nose. This is why an alarmed or interested horse will raise his head and point his nose where he is looking. You may have also noticed that when a horse is trying to focus on something relatively close (like when he is approaching and stepping into a trailer) he will often raise his head further from the subject. Because the horse sees independently with each eye, he has a very limited range within which both eyes can share a common focal point.

There is some evidence that the horse can see binocularly (as a human does, with depth perception) only a few meters in front of himself. If an object is too close, he must back away

to focus binocularly. This might explain why a horse spooks so easily, often shying from sudden movement that you can see is a safe distance away. The horse simply can't easily determine distances and may just shy at anything that moves anywhere in his field of vision.

The horse's long face and nose block a good portion of his field of vision and create a sizable blind spot directly in front of his nose. (Have you ever wondered how your horse can separate the corn from the oats in the bottom of a narrow bucket? The horse really cannot see what he's eating but has incredible "dexterity" in his lips that allows him to *feel* what he is eating. Bet you can't do that with *your* lips!) The blind spot in front of his nose might explain why an inexperienced trail horse can have so much trouble stepping over logs or other obstacles. He has to practice walking over things before his body knows what to do. By far the most common injury in the barn occurs when somebody has gotten his feet too near the horse's, and yet I've never known a horse to step on someone intentionally! A horse doesn't want to get on your feet—it's just that he is so big he can't always see what's underneath him.

The horse's wide body also creates a very large blind spot directly behind him, which is why you always want to approach a horse from an angle so you don't startle him. When you walk up to a horse, talk to him quietly and make your presence known.

The best horses often have physical characteristics that allow them to have exceptional binocular vision. Breeders and trainers have found that horses with eyes located toward the front of the face have considerably better vision than other horses, and many trainers use this factor as a major consideration in choosing prospects. Cutting, roping, and jumping horses depend largely on their binocular vision for tracking calves or locating a takeoff spot in front of the jump.

Cowboys have always avoided horses with a "dummy bump" between the eyes—those with eyes set way back on the sides of the face. They know that such a horse tends to be particularly spooky and excitable. An exceptionally high-headed horse can be uncomfortable and even dangerous to ride because his focal point and front field of vision is further away, while his blind spot is in the immediate foreground. Simply put, a high-headed horse often cannot see the ground right in front of his feet.

Most textbooks will tell you that horses are color-blind. I suspect that since the horse can't read, he doesn't know that he's not supposed to see colors! In research at one university, horses consistently "chose" grain buckets of a particular color from among various colored buckets. So maybe horses just see shades, as we do on a black and white television. Certainly red and blue and yellow would appear as recognizable

variations of grey, right? Yet, research horses were able to differentiate between light yellow and dark yellow when grain was moved from one bucket into another.

It is fairly certain that horses see colors much differently than humans do. For example, horses have trouble determining colors in very bright light but can determine colors in light too dim for humans. I believe horses see colors more clearly than most textbooks claim. Recently I replaced the dark green feed tubs in my stalls with new, fire-engine-red tubs. About a quarter of the horses went off their feed, and several wouldn't even go back into their stalls!

Horses Have Keen Hearing

What horses lack in vision, they make up for in hearing! A horse's ears can pivot nearly 180 degrees, allowing him to point them toward the source of any sound. Since each ear can turn and hear independently, the horse can detect very slight noises from separate directions simultaneously. A well-trained, attentive horse will nearly always have one ear turned back toward the rider while the other ear scans the area for other stimuli.

In many parts of the country, people like to hunt from horseback. Besides being able to cover more ground, hunters have learned to watch the ears of their horses for movement. Horses have much better hearing than humans and will turn their ears toward the source of a noise long before a human can detect the same sound. The horse can "point" out game before the hunter ever sees or hears it coming.

The acute hearing of the horse can be useful to the rider or trainer. We often use active voice aids in the early training of a horse because at that stage it is easier for a young colt to perceive

The ears are the window to the horse's mind. People love to see pretty horses with their ears perked forward, but when I'm riding I want to see his "listening ears" turned back toward me. This tells me he's paying attention.

Smells Communicate to a Horse

In the swamps that were home to prehistoric horses, an extremely keen sense of smell was developed to detect predators, identify companions or herd-mates, and find food. Today, wild stallions on the western ranges of the United States use their noses to figure out whether their herds are still on "home range," and domesticated horses have an equally acute sense of smell. You may have noticed some horses—especially stallions—smelling manure piles when you first turn them into a pasture. They can actually smell whether their friends have been turned out before them.

Maybe you have seen a horse sniff as you approach. Research suggests that horses can identify individual humans by their odor. In fact, recent research indicates that horses can smell very slight changes in the sweat glands of the skin, or maybe even hormonal changes caused by fear or excitement. This comes as no surprise to riders and teachers of riding who have long known that a horse can tell when a person is afraid.

and understand a voice aid than any other kind of cue. In fact, I often teach verbal commands to a colt before he is old enough to carry a rider. Most two-year-olds know "walk," "trot," and "whoa" from their work in the round pen or on the longe line before they are ever ridden.

Horses like for people to talk to them; they *don't* like people screaming into their sensitive, furry little ears. What's more, they don't understand more than a few words of anything you say but respond more to the tone and volume of your voice. A loud, abrasive rider can be as annoying to a horse as, say, a rap singer would be to me. A horse wants your voice to be quiet, soothing, reassuring. When giving commands or disciplinary correction, your voice should be firm and confident. Screaming or hollering just makes the horse upset.

Horses Have Wide Sensitivity to Touch

If you pay attention to how horses react in different situations, you have probably observed that they have a wide range of sensitivity to tactile stimuli. For example, most young horses are instinctively "head shy." A young horse must first learn to trust people before he will let himself be touched, particularly around the head.

On the other hand, do you know what part of the horse is the least sensitive to touch and has the lowest density of nerve endings? Let me answer that question with a question. Have you ever ridden a horse that seemed as though he couldn't even feel your legs on his sides? That's because the horse's sides have fewer nerve endings than any other fleshy area of his body. Ironically, we use our legs where he can least feel our cues! With a little use those nerve endings become even *less* sensitive. You don't need to wear spurs to ride well, but some horses definitely need to be ridden with them, no doubt about it!

The horse's mouth also has a relatively low density of nerve endings. (That's why it can be so easy to ruin a horse's mouth—he can't afford to lose many of them!) As a result, I always recommend doing early, high-contact training with a very mild bit. Many trainers, particularly in the stock-seat discipline and in the western regions of this country, will break and train horses in a bosal. (A bosal, sometimes called a hackamore, is a type of bridle that isolates rein pressure on the horse's nose and underbars of the jaw rather than in the mouth.) That way, they are not even touching the horse's mouth during training. Once the horse is fairly well trained, they switch to a bit.

Well then, if the sides and the mouth are not very sensitive, what part of the horse *is*? One very sensitive area is his back. Have you ever noticed how a horse can feel even a small fly on his back and twitch a little to get rid of him? Sensitivity in this area is what makes the use of seat and weight aids so effective. The horse can be trained to respond to very minor changes in the pressure and position of the rider's seat. These cues can be a real advantage for a good rider, but often they become an annoyance for the horse carrying a rider who's flopping around like a carp on his back.

The withers are another sensitive area and are an ideal place to communicate reassurance and trust to the horse. Many trainers like to pat or massage the horse on the withers in a tense situation or as a reward at the end of a successful training session. The next time your horse gets tense and starts to trot too fast, loosen your reins, try a half-seat or two-point, and rub his withers or neck. Trust your horse for a couple of minutes. He might relax and decide to trot slowly.

The withers and lower neck are sensitive enough to be used in neck reining, whereby the horse is trained to respond to the feel of the rein against these areas. An advanced Western horse may become so tuned in to the feel of reins on his neck that you never need to use a bit in his mouth.

Horses Have Intuition

In addition to vision, hearing, smell, touch, and taste, horses seem to have a sixth sense, as well: they have an uncanny ability to pick up on your moods. Like a dog, your horse knows if you are nervous, happy, angry, naughty or nice, whatever. If you aren't relaxed and confident, the horse will sense this immediately and usually responds by being high strung or stubborn. (If nothing else, he can smell your uncertainty!)

In riding classes, it seems as though the nervous riders always get the difficult horses. The truth is, any horse the nervous rider gets can sense his apprehension and tries to misbehave. In beginning lessons I often see horses just playing, testing to see how much they can get away with. If you are nervous about horses, try to become self-assured and commanding. Only then will the horse believe you.

THE HORSE'S BODY LANGUAGE

You know your horse better than anyone else. If he acts unhappy, there must be a reason for his unhappiness, and it's your job to figure out what it is. Like humans, horses exhibit body language that indicates moods or attitude. Generally speaking, a horse carries his ears forward when he is comfortable and interested in his task. Most people know that when a horse lays his ears back, he is not a happy camper. But such a response is not the same as when the horse turns his ears to focus on something behind him. When I am training, I want to see his "listening ears" turned toward me when I am communicating with him. If the horse pins his ears in anger, you'll know it! Trust me on this.

I like for a horse to carry his tail flat and quiet. You can tell a horse doesn't like what he's doing if his tail is constantly twitching. I've seen horses that will crank their tail at every jump, or every time they're asked to do a flying change of lead. A horse that carries his tail up high might have some discomfort in his back or the way the rider is sitting on his back.

The horse is the best riding teacher you can have. If you are doing something wrong, he usually lets you know it. For example, a horse that moves stiffly or is short-strided might resent the aids he's receiving. When your horse isn't being cooperative, it may be helpful to watch somebody else ride him—somebody really good. He might exhibit different body language with another rider, clueing you in to what's bothering him.

TEACHING YOUR HORSE

When training horses, we need to remember that horses are not terribly intelligent. If they were, jumping horses would have figured out by now that they can simply jump the pasture gate rather than wait for someone to open it for them! The only way to teach a horse is through repetition and discipline, and most of his initial reactions are instinctive. However, I think horses are smarter than most animals because they are easily trained to simple command-response stimuli.

The Horse's Memory

Horses seem to have very good memory. Before you throw this book into the manure pile in disbelief, answer this: Have you ever had a horse that had a really bad experience in a trailer? I have, and it is very tough to get him back into that trailer. Some horses won't forget something like that for the rest of their lives. That's just an example, but you can probably recall a similar experience. Maybe it's clippers that set him off. Farriers? Motorcycles? On the plus side, you can get on an old horse that hasn't been ridden in years, and—providing he was well trained—he probably won't need more than a ride or two before he remembers most everything he ever knew.

My friend had a horse who would nicker every time he turned into the driveway after a show. It was his way of welcoming himself home after a long weekend. Eventually, my friend moved to another farm, but after several years he visited the old place with the horse in the trailer behind him. You guessed it! The horse recognized the driveway and nickered just as he had done years before.

Memory has also played an important role in the survival of the horse. For example, in the arid West of North America, wild bands of horses didn't just stumble upon watering holes by accident. It's believed that a horse ranking high in the social order of a herd was responsible for remembering directions and leading the rest of the herd to water.

The Learned Instinct

The theory behind all horse training is the same: when the animal responds to an uncomfortable stimulus with the desired response, he is given a

"I can catch him—Horses ain't that smart."

comfortable reprieve. We use a variety of cues to communicate with the horse, and he knows that if he responds appropriately, the rider will stop using the cue. I call this the "learned instinct," one on which I base my entire training method.

Horsemanship is about reinforcing the horse's positive responses, so that over time he is trained to refine his predictable behavior. Let's say you are cruising along at a canter and your cellular phone rings, so you want to stop. You pull on the reins, which activates the pressure points of the bit. The horse's learned instinct is to back away from the pressure in his mouth. The bit is causing an uncomfortable stimulus, but the horse remembers that if he stops in this situation the rider will release the pressure in his mouth. This is how a horse learns—he responds to end the uncomfortable stimulus caused by the rider.

Contrary to what most people like to think about a horse wanting to please his master, a horse responds properly to make himself more comfortable! But here's the catch: He has to remember the appropriate response to that particular cue. That's why we try to simplify training as much as possible, making it easy for the horse to succeed. For example, when teaching a horse to move away from leg pressure, I won't ask him to move *toward* the rail until he's first learned the psychologically easier variation of the movement—moving *away* from the rail.

The Correlation Response

A primary goal in equitation is to ride "quietly," which in part means using the least severe cue

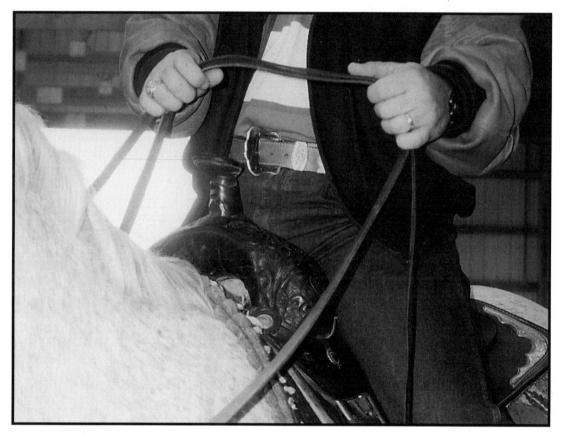

The horse feels the neck rein on the right side first, followed by a left leading rein. He eventually learns to respond to the more comfortable neck rein to avoid the second aid.

you can. Sometimes it's a primary aid applied with less intensity (for example, a squeeze of the leg rather than a kick.) To ride even more quietly, we can sometimes teach the horse to relate the less severe *secondary* aid to the more severe primary aid that follows. Then after a period of training we can rely mostly on the secondary aids.

Let's go back to the scenario where you are cantering along and need to stop. Typically, you begin every downward transition with the half-halt of the active seat and the voice aid "whoa"—both of which are secondary aids. Eventually when you settle down to the seat and say "whoa," your horse knows that the more severe primary aid (the rein aid) is about to follow. He responds

quickly to the secondary aids to save himself the discomfort of the primary aid.

This example illustrates the second and more advanced way in which horses learn, which I call the "correlation response." The horse first learns an appropriate response to a primary stimulus, based on his learned instincts. Then a secondary stimulus is introduced just before the primary cue. In time, the secondary stimulus *becomes* the primary cue because you can discontinue what once was the original primary cue.

Neck reining is a good example of the correlation response. Typically, a young horse is well established in direct reining before he learns to neck rein. At some point in the horse's development, the trainer begins to neck rein immediately before giving his direct rein cue. Eventually the horse discovers the correlation and begins responding to the neck rein, at which point the direct rein stimulus becomes unnecessary and is dropped completely.

The key to this type of learning is to always apply the correlating aid (the secondary stimulus) *before* the established primary cue. Eventually the horse learns to respond to the secondary stimulus without waiting for the primary cue. This is precisely how a horse graduates, little by little, from basic to more advanced training. In this way, horse training is a matter of building and relating, starting with simple concepts and refining them into complex responses.

Basic Truths a Trainer Must Know

If training a horse were as easy as I make it sound in this chapter, anybody could do it and we wouldn't need the professionals. No doubt there is some natural talent and instinct involved, but these fundamental truths about training can be applied to horses no matter what your level of skill.

1. First, it takes a special kind of patience to be a good horse trainer. Horse training takes time— more time than many people are willing to spend. Don't be discouraged if you don't see the immediate or spectacular results that you expected. Always remember that your success depends on the trust you can establish with any given horse. Anything that undermines that trust will ultimately diminish your chances of seeing effective results. The most common mistake is to lose your temper, and the next most common is to push a horse to advance faster than he is capable of progressing.

2. The second thing you need to understand from the start is that you absolutely cannot *make* the horse do anything he doesn't want to do. The challenge in training a horse is to be cunning enough to charm him into trusting and working with you. A horse trainer is a cross between a lover and a fighter, a psychologist and an athletic coach. You have to be brave and strong and stubborn enough to impart some firm and immediate discipline when the horse decides to resist. Losing your temper doesn't help. When things start going badly and getting really stressful, good trainers have the ability to stay calm and think clearly about what can help the situation at hand. Since there is no way you can out-muscle an animal ten times your size, you've got to make the horse want what you want.

3. The third training truth is that although there is no single, superior way to train horses, all the successful trainers I've known have based their training methods on classical theories of horsemanship. They might not use the same words I do to describe their techniques, but inevitably they employ the same fundamental concepts. This common thread in training is the basis of my mental equitation philosophy. If you strip away the frills of the various riding styles, you'll find very similar methods being used in Western pleasure, hunter equitation, and reining barns. Don't be confused by semantics; instead, educate yourself enough to recognize the mechanics of a training system even when the labels are different.

Tricks of the Trade

While there is no magical short cut to horse training, the following advice can help you make the most of your time and effort:

• *Know when to say when.* Students sometimes brag to me that they spent two hours riding and training, or three hours practicing their equitation. Did you know that professional horse trainers rarely spend more than a half-hour at a time on a horse? Many trainers will quit on a horse after ten or fifteen minutes if training is going well. I rarely ask my riders to practice equitation for longer than that. Think about human athletic training. Any good baseball coach knows that once a batter gets tired, he can't deliver the hits he normally would.

As a trainer, you need to do any serious teaching while the horse is fresh and attentive. When a horse becomes tired or distracted, your time is best spent on physical conditioning. Frequent, brief training sessions are always better than infrequent, lengthy sessions—for riders as well as for horses.

• *Make sure the horse enjoys training.* I'm not saying that you shouldn't make corrections, just don't make training such drudgery that the horse won't want to come out of the barn next time. Change focus occasionally, introduce something new. Avoid the tendency to keep repeating the things that he already does well; likewise, don't dwell on weaknesses too long. Offer your horse a kind word when he cooperates or a pat on the neck when he succeeds. When I am riding and training, I like to stop my horse and let him stand occasionally. It rewards him for doing well by giving him a little rest while also teaching him some self-discipline.

• *Give your horse time to warm up and cool down.* It's unreasonable to expect immediate concentration as soon as a horse enters the ring. If you're feeding him well, and he's strong and fit, your horse is going to need time to blow off some steam. Start by letting him work off his playfulness on

the end of a longe line or in a round pen.

Once you're mounted, give him a long rein and let him loosen up at a long, relaxed trot. Most of us don't go "hell-bent for leather" the instant we step onto a racquetball court, so we shouldn't expect our horses to do the equivalent. After four or five minutes of stretching and loosening up, your horse will be relaxed and you will sense that he's ready to work. Now's the ideal time to teach him something new, so don't waste the opportunity!

It's equally important to let your horse cool off after you finish your ride. To help horses unwind mentally as well as physically, many trainers like to take them out of the arena and into a field or on a trail or farm road.

• *Teach your horse self-discipline.* Horses need to know that there's a time to work and a time to play. For example, they need to know that when wearing a saddle and bridle, it is unacceptable to reach down and try to eat grass. Nor is it all right to interact with other horses in the arena. One of the things that aggravates me most is the "school horse" mentality, like when one horse leaves the schooling ring and your horse thinks it's time to quit. Or when the horse's internal clock tells him it's feeding time and he can't concentrate on anything else.

I once managed a stallion that was more interested in feeding than breeding! (Actually, I guess the same could be said for some people.) We had to arrange our breedings so they didn't fall too near his feeding time, or he simply wouldn't get the job done. We finally figured out that instead of accommodating him, we should vary his routine so he didn't have a routine anymore. Eventually, he learned to deal with distractions and became a much better lover.

Don't cater to your horse! You don't have to break your neck to feed or turn him out at *exactly* the same time every day. He can wait a few minutes. Make your horse deal with life's little annoyances just like you do. People still keep horses in tie stalls successfully, and cowboys still hobble horses in some situations. That tells me that horses can have patience and manners if you teach them. I know a trainer who will intentionally take a horse away from his breakfast or lunch just to teach him self-control and show him there are other things more important than food.

I have seen horses pampered to a point that their genetic toughness and resilience have been worn away by over-mothering. Some people won't turn a horse out because they're afraid he'll hurt himself by running too hard, or because they don't want the horse breathing the cold air. Listen, that's what horses do—run and breath hard! They are athletes and *need* to exercise. Horses are stronger, smarter, and more resilient than most people realize, and it's been my experience that the sickest, lamest horses are usually the ones that are coddled the most.

If you're going to ride very much, you must accept that sometimes you will do everything right and training still won't go well. Once you know how to ask the horse properly, you can usually get him to do the things you want him to do—but not always. This goes back to what sets riding apart from other sports: the personality of a willful partner. Sometimes he'll be playful and not want to work. Or, he may just be in a bad mood (that happens to me sometimes, too). A horse has a changing temperament, just like you and me.

Without question, some trainers can get more from a horse than others. Every trainer has his own system of feeding, fitting, disciplining, and preparing horses for competition. These are all environmental factors that have a definite bearing on a horse's ability to reach his potential. Exceptional trainers are real professionals, with a special skill or talent that not everyone has. However, mental equitation can help most riders accomplish "maintenance training," which goes on for the entire life of the horse.

If you don't ride your horse often enough to keep him quiet, you may end up spending two-thirds of every ride fighting his nervous energy. Before you ride, a little free-longeing in a round pen like this one can save you both a lot of anxiety. This guy isn't mean, just playful!

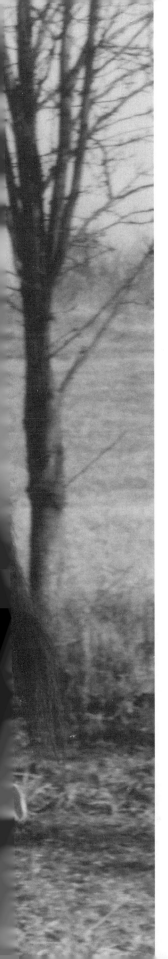

 CHAPTER THREE

EVALUATING A HORSE'S POTENTIAL FOR SUCCESS

Depending on your riding discipline, you may be looking for a horse that has a particular aptitude. A person who knows a little about conformation has a good chance of selecting a prospect that will do a job effectively. For example, you wouldn't want to choose a reining horse with a heavy head and neck and a weak hind end, because stopping and backing could be a constant struggle against mother nature!

Although most horses can be improved by someone with talent and knowledge—a fact that keeps professional trainers in business—you can't make a champion unless he has the goods. You have to discover that kind of talent, and you never know where you might find it. I know a woman who was an alternate for the American team at the most recent Pan-American Games, and she got her dressage horse out of a wild herd out West someplace. World Champion Charmayne Rodman rescued her legendary barrel horse, "Scamper," from a killer lot. And "John Henry," one of the greatest racehorses in history, was sold for next to nothing after a short and ordinary racing career. Although he was supposed to have been washed up, the new owners gelded him, and he raced for another decade, breaking all records for career earnings. The hope that you might discover the next world champion under unlikely circumstances is what keeps the horse business going.

I once had the privilege to work for Lee Eaton during Thoroughbred sales at Keeneland and Fasig-Tipton in Lexington, Kentucky. Eaton, a very successful Kentucky sales agent, is the most talented person I have ever known when it comes to evaluating a horse's conformation. During a sixty-second showing on the morning of a sale, Eaton could see more in a horse than most people would ever see. No doubt such people have a natural talent for assessing conformation and mechanics, but it is also a skill that's improved with study and practice.

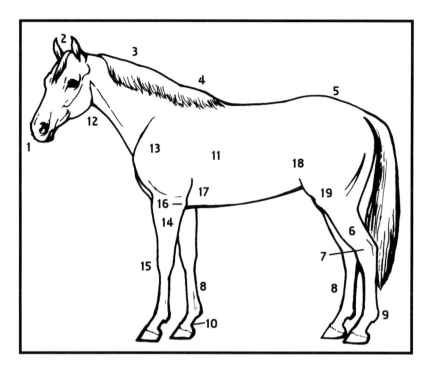

Parts of the Horse

1. muzzle
2. poll
3. crest
4. withers
5. croup
6. gaskin
7. hock
8. cannon
9. fetlock
10. pastern
11. barrel
12. throatlatch
13. shoulder
14. forearm
15. knee
16. elbow
17. girth
18. flank
19. stifle

CONFORMATION

Conformation is the structural configuration of the horse's body, including the length, mass, angles, and balance of the skeletal and muscular components. Like an "equine mechanical engineer," someone with a trained eye can spot conformation assets or problems that will make a horse more or less likely to achieve success. That person can often predict, based on conformation, characteristics of a horse's movement and potential for injury.

The Hindquarters Assembly

If you watch a horse running and then stopping, you will see that his strength comes from the hindquarters. He doesn't *pull* himself forward; the forehand is mostly just a balancing and steering mechanism. The hindquarters always provide the power. I like to think of the horse as being like an old Volkswagen Beetle, with an engine in the back and the steering in the front. To get lateral movement from the horse you steer his front end, but you get forward impulsion from the engine in the rear. With the power coming up underneath, the steering is light and responsive (much *unlike* the VW "Bug" I drove through college). I talk about this especially when I am working with jumpers, but the concept applies to all disciplines.

A horse with a bigger, more muscular rear end tends to be more centrally balanced and athletic in events that require a lot of power in the hindquarters, such as jumping or reining. However, since most riding disciplines require less than maximum rear-end thrust, a moderately muscled hindquarter is usually sufficient.

The angle of the croup (or area across the topline between the back and the tail) is a concern for many disciplines because it indicates the angle of the horse's pelvis and the origin of his

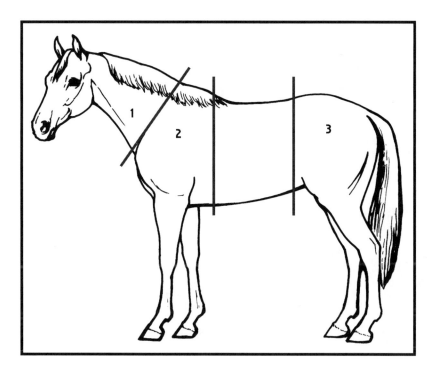

hip joint. This information can suggest how long- or short-strided the horse might be, particularly if the croup is exceptionally steep or flat. An old racetracker once told me that distance horses should be flat across the croup, while sprinters should have a steeper croup and a larger rear end. It makes sense that distance horses need a longer, freer stride, while powerful hindquarters are more important to the sprinter. You may have noticed that racehorses at Quarter Horse tracks don't look quite like Thoroughbreds, even though they're bred from largely Thoroughbred stock. That's because breeders have learned how to blend the Thoroughbred stride with the powerful Quarter Horse hindquarter assembly.

The Forehand Assembly

Another racetrack rule of thumb is that sprinters should have "low knees"—in other words,

short cannons, with minimal lower leg breakover time in every stride. This is a desirable character- istic for horses that need to have quick feet (especially high-performance horses like cutters or reiners). Short cannons are a *dis*advantage to horses that need to have a long stride.

You should be getting the picture by now that sprinters tend to be built like Quarter Horses, with a conformation that lends itself to quick, athletic, and explosive movement over short distances. Distance horses are invariably built like Thorough- breds, with longer legs, a longer and more lightly muscled back, and more lightly muscled hind- quarters. Horses having this conformation get off to a slower start, but have more stamina and speed in the long run, as seen in a hunter or even the modern Western pleasure horse.

A long forearm and gaskin are desirable for all types of horses because they give the horse leverage, power, and length in his stride. Long forearms typically make a horse fast, strong,

The horse uses his head and neck to balance as he moves. The intensity of balancing gestures indicates the degree of natural balance within a gait, with the trot being the most balanced and canter being the least balanced.

athletic, and graceful, especially when combined with short cannons.

The horse has no clavicle, or collarbone. His scapula, or shoulder blade, is attached to the rest of his body only by tendons and muscle. Anatomically, this arrangement helps to disperse and soften impact through the leg. If the horse's forearms were attached to the body through a collarbone (the way arms are in humans), the stress on the bones in his front legs would be unbearable.

The angle of the shoulder also affects the impact of stride. A straight-shouldered horse has a scapula that runs more vertically from the withers to the shoulder joint and tends to have a very bouncy, jolting stride. Because a straight-shouldered horse also has the ball-and-socket shoulder joint set further back beneath him than is desirable, he will often be particularly prone to injury in the front end.

The Head and Neck Assembly

The weight of the head and neck (or the angle at which the neck is set into the shoulder) can greatly affect a horse's natural head carriage, and therefore directly affects his longitudinal balance. (I will explain more about longitudinal balance in Chapter 7.) A horse with a neck set high into the shoulder cannot carry his head at a normal or low head position and tends to have a vertical center of balance that is further back than average. This can be a useful trait for a roping horse or even a jumper if the head is not so high that it prohibits normal vision.

A horse with a very large or heavy head and neck (or a neck set low into the shoulder) will be heavy on the forehand and have trouble engaging his weight on the hindquarters. This is the reputation Quarter Horses had in the hunter world for many years. The modern Quarter Horse is generally more refined, taller, and more acceptable as a hunter.

Desirable in most disciplines is a horse with a long, thin neck, which helps the horse balance himself. A trim throatlatch is desirable in all disciplines, since a horse with a thick throat has trouble flexing at the poll and may even have trouble breathing when flexed to the bit.

MOVEMENT AND THE HORSE'S CENTER OF BALANCE

Each horse has a natural center of balance that is dependent on his size and weight, conformation and proportions, etc. The center of balance can also be affected by the activity in which he is engaged, and by the skill of the rider in creating the most effective center of balance for that activity. The center of balance is the point on the horse's body at which we could theoretically lift him by a string and he would be balanced front to rear, like a mobile. In general, a horse will have a center of balance just behind his withers,

which moves further forward as he increases speed, or backward during activities that require lateral agility.

Static Balance

Although a horse will often compensate for faults when he is in motion, his imperfections are often revealed when he is standing still. If you don't have a horse handy, you can refer to the one in the illustration. I have drawn a vertical line (center of mechanical motion) halfway between his front and rear legs, thus dividing the body mass supported by each set of legs. Due to the weight of his head and neck, a horse's front legs carry approximately sixty percent of his total body weight, explaining why most leg injuries and soundness problems involve the horse's front legs and feet.

Whatever his conformation, a horse standing still will find a way to be balanced. In his wonderful

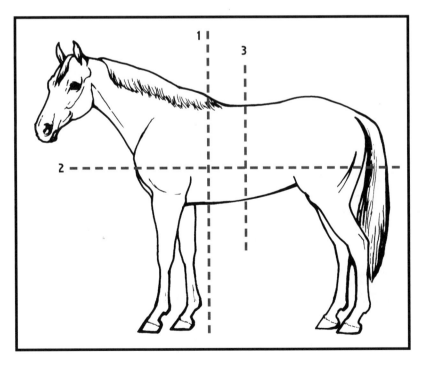

Static Balance

1. Vertical Center of Balance

2. Horizontal Center of Balance

3. Center of Mechanical Motion

The horse's "center of balance" is the point at which he is balanced from front to rear. Here he is shown at "static balance," or standing still. Notice that the vertical center of balance is not the center of his body.

book, *Riding and Schooling the Western Performance Horse,* Dr. G. F. Corley called this the principle of "static balance." Since static balance is fairly easy for most horses to achieve, you probably should reconsider your dreams of winning a world championship if your horse has trouble with it!

When you observe a horse that is standing still, notice how he positions his head and neck. Is he naturally high headed? Is the neck set very high into the shoulder? Is he ewe necked? Notice the placement of his rear legs under the hindquarters. As I explained earlier, the angle and length of the croup affect a horse's ability to engage the hindquarters.

Now look at the horse at static balance and imagine the point on his back at which he could dangle from a string and be balanced front to back. This "vertical center of balance" will be somewhere just behind his withers. It is not the center of his mechanical motion because of the weight of the horse's head. This is why draft horse breeds don't usually make ideal riding horses: The heavier the head and neck, the further forward you will find his vertical center of balance. A smaller head and thinner neck are more desirable for most breeds, because that combination places the center of balance further back toward the middle of the horse, encouraging engagement of the hindquarters and lightness in the front end.

The vertical center of balance is remarkably close to the point at which the saddle is balanced on a saddle tree. If you balance a saddle on your fist, you will find that its center of balance is not in the center of the saddle; rather, its balance is centered near the front.

Now draw an imaginary line through the vertical center of balance on the horse at static balance. Imagine a saddle on the horse, and draw an imaginary line through the center of balance for the saddle. Finally, imagine a rider in two-point position, and draw an imaginary line through her

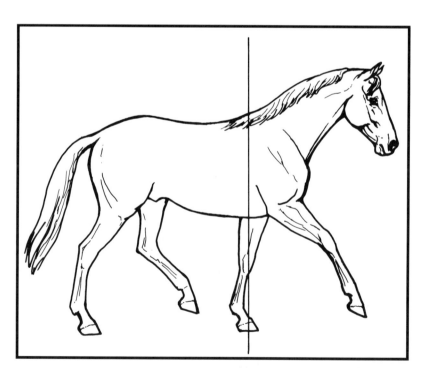

Dynamic Balance

The horse's center of balance in motion at the trot. Notice it is further forward than the static center of balance in the previous drawing. As the horse moves in a faster gait, the center of balance tends to be carrried further forward.

"Dynamic balance" is the recurrent loss and regaining of balance on every stride. You can see how this horse is balanced on the second beat of the canter. In the next instant, he will drop his head and lose his balance forward, before recapturing his balance on his right front or "lead" foot. As a rule, the faster the horse goes, the further forward is his center of balance. As a result, a rider sits more forward in faster gaits. *A. Kumekawa photo.*

center of balance. All three imaginary lines should line up side by side, as shown on page 25.

Dynamic Balance

If you haven't done so lately, spend a little time standing by the fence of the turnout lot, watching horses play and run. This is the best place to observe the horse's natural movements, which are often different than their show ring movements. (Sometimes it is much easier to distinguish between good and bad movers when a rider isn't getting in the way.) You can learn a lot about a horse's potential for success by watching him unrestricted in play.

If a horse is a pretty mover in the pasture, you can bet he'll move nicely in the arena. However, don't lose heart if your favorite colt isn't the prettiest mover. Unless he has some conformational fault that makes him hopelessly clumsy, a good rider can greatly improve his movement. Through effective use of natural aids, a good rider can manipulate the horse's lateral and longitudinal agility to create a more desirable way of going. That's what mental equitation is all about—a broad understanding that gives you the power to tinker.

V. S. Littauer, a student of horsemanship theories whose works were in print in the early twentieth century, was the first to point out that the horse's center of balance changes from one moment to the next as he moves. He realized that the forward movement of the horse is not only the result of the powerful actions of the hindquarters, but also represents recurrent loss and subsequent regaining of equilibrium to the front. He called this concept of changing equilibrium "dynamic balance."

This shift in balance is easiest to visualize if you imagine a man walking. As he shifts his weight forward, he loses his balance momentarily but then regains it on the forward foot. The forward foot then becomes the back foot as he moves his other foot ahead, and so on. Walking is a constant losing and regaining of balance from the rear to the fore. The larger the stride, the more pronounced is the loss of balance. (Based on this theory, I have a more balanced stride than Shaquille O'Neal!)

The forward motion of a horse also consists of alternating periods of balance and imbalance. A horse uses his head and neck to maintain his balance in much the same way a man swings his arms. "Balance" is the horse's ability to deal gracefully and efficiently with this ongoing phenomenon. More specifically, a horse that is balanced has learned to deal with his own center of balance and that of the rider. A horse that is not balanced tends to carry his head a little low and very stiff through the poll and neck, moving stiffly in front and disengaged behind.

BASIC MECHANICS OF MOTION

To visualize how a horse's balance changes through a stride, you need to first understand his footfall patterns. The footfall patterns represent the most

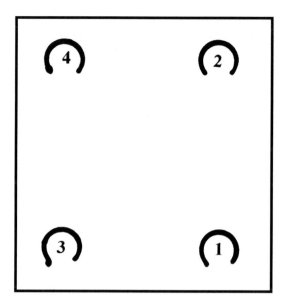

The WALK is a four-beat lateral gait in which each foot strikes the ground independently of the others. No matter which foot you begin with, the sequence is always the same.

basic mechanics of motion. Understanding how a horse cycles through a stride will allow you to visualize how a horse's balance changes through the stride, and how he can "link" these footfall patterns in a transition of gait.

The Walk

The walk is a four-beat gait consisting of a continuous pattern of rear-front on one side followed by rear-front on the other side. In other words, the footfall pattern is right-rear, right-front, left-rear, left-front, and so on. At any point in the sequence, the horse should have three feet on the ground and one foot up. The horse's four feet always move in this order.

The motion of the horse's head and neck indicate how much effort is required to maintain balance in each gait. Typically, the horse bobs his head somewhat while he walks, suggesting that

Foot position on beat number one of the four-beat WALK, as the left-rear foot strikes the ground. It continues . . .

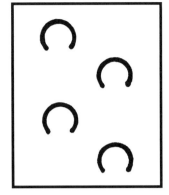

Foot position on beat number two of the four-beat WALK, as the left-front foot strikes the ground.

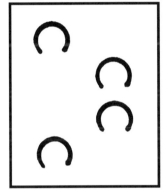

Foot position on beat number three of the four-beat WALK, as the right-rear foot strikes the ground.

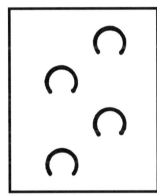

Foot position on beat number four of the four-beat WALK, as the right-front foot strikes the ground. This continuous, repeating sequence never changes.

he must use his head moderately to keep himself balanced. Because of the horse's wide basis for balance, the walk is a fairly balanced gait. The loss of balance is due primarily to the footfall sequence that requires him to shift laterally on every other beat while he is simultaneously shifting horizontally.

The Trot

The trot is a continuous, two-beat, diagonal gait, with opposite diagonal feet pairing for each beat. In other words, the left-rear and right-front feet hit the ground at the same time, and then the right-rear and left-front feet come down simultaneously.

Because of the diagonal pairs, the trot is a

A nice, balanced English trot. Notice that balancing movements of the head are minimal in the trot, compared to other gaits.

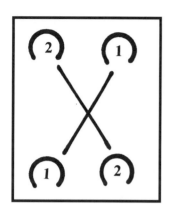

The TROT is a 2-beat diagonal gait, with the opposite corners moving as pairs on the same beat of the gait.

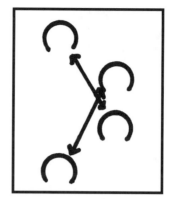

Foot position on beat number one of the 2-beat TROT, as the right-rear and left-front diagonal pair strikes the ground. It continues . . .

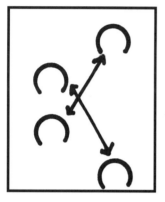

Foot position on beat number two of the 2-beat TROT, as the left-rear and right-front diagonal pair strikes the ground. This continuous, repeating sequence never changes.

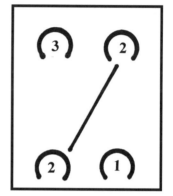

The CANTER is a three-beat gait, with the diagonal pair falling on beat 2, and a period of suspension following beat 3.

very balanced gait. The horse always has one foot from each end and each side of his body on the ground. The pelvic girdle and shoulders work opposite one another, rhythmically and repeatedly, in the same recurring two-beat sequence. You can tell from watching the balancing gestures of the head and neck that this is the most balanced of the three natural gaits. Think of how it feels to sit a trot. Can you feel the horse's outside hip and inside shoulder lifting at the same time? You should be able to feel your hips moving laterally as the horse's spine twists.

The Canter

The canter is a three-beat gait with constantly changing balance. The horse balances briefly on a single outside rear foot on beat one, the diagonal pair of feet hits the ground on beat two, a leading leg touches down on beat three, and a period of suspension follows, when all four feet are off the ground simultaneously. (At least, this is theoretically true. In a very slow canter, all four feet might not be off the ground at the same time.)

The first beat of the cycle, following suspension, is when the horse steps down with the outside-rear foot. This is the *least* balanced point in the canter, quickly followed by beat two, when the diagonal pair of inside-rear and outside-fore feet touch down. This moment is the *most* balanced point in the canter, because three feet are on the ground at once. Finally, the leading foot contacts the ground on beat three, followed by the period of suspension.

The canter shifts the horse's balance vertically

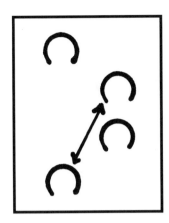

Foot position on beat number one of the three-beat CANTER on the left lead, as the right-rear foot strikes the ground. It continues . . .

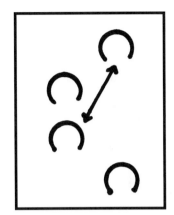

Foot position on beat number two of the three-beat CANTER on the left lead, as the left-rear and right-front diagonal pair strikes the ground.

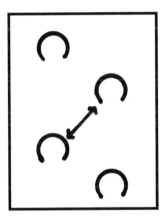

Foot position on beat number three of the three-beat CANTER on the left lead, as the left-front (lead) foot strikes the ground. This continuous, repeating sequence is always the same.

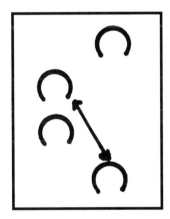

You could work out the corresponding sequence for the canter on the right lead. Here's the first beat . . .

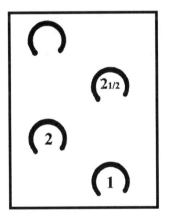

The sequence of the four-beat GALLOP is a little different than the canter.

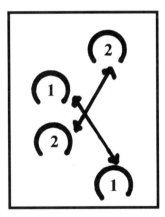

The sequence for the BACK is like the trot in reverse, two beats of diagonal pairs continuously repeating.

In beat one of the canter, the horse is balanced on the outside rear leg. The rider is in the forward "hip closed" position as the horse raises the forehand.

A nice balanced canter on the left lead. The second beat of the canter—when the diagonal pair is on the ground—is the most balanced point in the canter cycle.

as well. As the cycle begins, part of the horse's weight comes down onto the outside-rear foot. Most of the weight is still suspended and won't settle until beat two, when the diagonal pair and outside-rear foot carry the horse's weight and the downward force of the momentum. Think about the up-and-down, rocking motion of the canter. Beat two is the point at which momentum drops your weight into the saddle. As the leading foot comes down on beat three, the outside-rear foot disengages behind, and the downward force of the weight and momentum briefly rests on the leading foot and the diagonal pair.

When the diagonal pair disengages backward and the outside-rear foot begins to engage forward in the air, the momentum is carried forward and down, and all the force comes down on the single leading leg. (This explains why most leg injuries and unsoundnesses occur in the horse's front legs. Racehorse research has shown that a horse's front leg absorbs about 5,000 pounds of downward force on the third beat of the gallop!) Finally, as the leading leg disengages backward, the horse begins the period of suspension when all legs are briefly off the ground. This

Balanced with all weight moving forward onto the leading leg at the end of beat three, the horse is probably carrying more than a ton of pressure on that foot! The rider is sitting up in the "hip open" position. In an instant, the whole cycle begins again.

is when you feel as though you are floating upward out of the saddle.

Because of a footfall sequence that shifts weight both forward and laterally at the same time, the canter is the least balanced gait, as indicated by the exaggerated balancing gestures of the horse's head and neck.

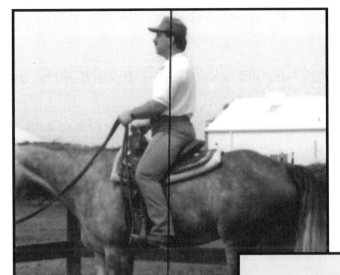

Left: Compare this handsome young rider to the hunt seat and you can see that the interdisciplinary nature of proper equitation disciplines perceive each other as different functions—but we all use the same means to achieve those ends.

Right: "Sitting on the pockets," or too heavy onto the tail bone, puts the rider behind the motion. Compare this shoulder-to-hip line to the imaginary vertical. You can see the rider is compensating by pushing his facial hair to the wind in an attempt to regain balance.

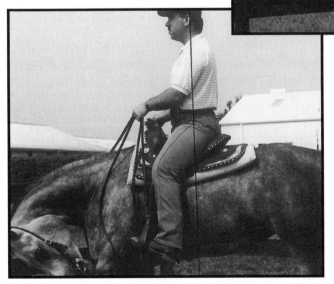

Left: If you force the heel down, the knee straightens, taking the lower leg off the imaginary vertical.

31

BREEDING AND HEREDITY

When selecting a horse for a particular kind of riding, it's wise to look for one that has the best possible genetic chance for success. Horse breeders have worked for centuries to produce the right combinations of physical strength, intelligence, and heart that make champions like "Secretariat." There are always exceptions, but breeders and trainers know that the best predictor for success often boils down to heredity.

Without question, certain breeds and even certain bloodlines within a breed are known for special characteristics. For example, Arabians are known for toughness, soundness, and endurance. Thoroughbreds are famous for speed and wind. The American Quarter Horse is known for quickness and strength. Within the Quarter Horse breed, "Impressive" lines are known for beauty and structure, "Doc Bar" for agility and cow sense, "Go Man Go" for incredible speed, and so on.

A smart horse owner or breeder studies and selects bloodlines appropriate for certain tasks. Although I would never suggest that genetics is an exact science (there are successes and failures in every breeding program), the best sires and dams can reproduce predictable physical characteristics with remarkable accuracy and results.

Just a few decades ago, somebody decided to breed small horses together in an attempt to produce even smaller horses. Today the product is a horse, proportional in every way, that you have to reach down to pat on the back! The point is, a small group of miniature horse breeders went to work selecting and rebreeding for clearly defined characteristics, creating a very impressive product in a relatively short period of time.

The Tennessee Walking Horse is another product of selective breeding. Developed in the American South prior to the Civil War, the Tennessee Walker was designed to be a comfortable touring mount for plantation owners. In the characteristic "running walk," the horse drops his hip and moves almost entirely on the hindquarters. It typically has a massive rear end and steep croup, and a very short and highly set neck that allows him to get his head up and shift weight backward more easily.

Unfortunately, for every attribute we can breed into a horse, we tend to lose something else. For example, the Thoroughbred is undeniably the most suitable breed for races of a mile or more. A century of meticulous breeding has accomplished exactly what breeders wanted. However, I have found that Thoroughbreds are much harder to settle in foal and much more likely to need help foaling than other breeds. This is because they are usually narrow in the pelvis and thoracic cavity relative to their overall size and the size of their babies. This type of build can restrict certain loops of the digestive system, as well, causing Thoroughbreds to colic more often and more severely than other breeds.

By now you have probably concluded that you could spend most of your life looking for the perfect horse. Each of the factors discussed in this chapter might increase your odds for success, but you need to decide which ones are the most important for your endeavors and how much perfection you need. Then be diligent in searching for those qualities.

Obviously, the most overall perfect horses are also the most expensive. In my days with Lee Eaton I learned that, while some buyers are lucky enough to find a bargain champion, most spend too much on potential that never pans out. Mental equitation will help you understand and focus on what is really important to you. If you find the horse that is right for you and has the most important factors for your riding discipline, buy him.

At the Western canter (or "lope"), the horse is centrally balanced, with a low and relaxed head carriage. The canter is the least balanced gait, as indicated by the active balancing gestures of the head and neck.

Compare the mechanics and balance of Ollie's gallop to my Western Pleasure canter. Can you see that this horse is lighter on his front end, partly because of his head carriage? Notice he's going in a bosal.

CHAPTER FOUR

COMMUNICATING WITH THE HORSE THROUGH NATURAL AIDS

Mental equitation involves more than simply riding a horse. To ride well, the rider must *communicate* with the horse, using his body or other aids to send messages that the horse is trained to understand. Since each horse has his own quirks or habits, the rider must analyze the horse's movements in order to respond appropriately. This is what mental equitation is all about.

Learning equitation is like learning a foreign language. It is possible to get by if you merely memorize key phrases and words, but you really can't speak the language until you know how to use the words in conversation. Similarly, mental equitation supplies the understanding you need to "talk" to your horse, using natural or artificial aids.

Natural aids are those methods of communicating with the horse that involve the rider's hands, legs, seat, and voice. In contrast, artificial aids are *not* a natural part of the rider; these include whips, spurs, martingales, tie-downs, head-setters, and leg-chains. Artificial aids are not necessarily bad. They have a place in horsemanship, but it is important to understand that artificial aids should be used to supplement, not substitute for, natural aids.

Good professional trainers use very few artificial aids. Most trainers ride with spurs, and some English trainers routinely carry a crop, but not because of a deficiency in their natural aids. They supplement their natural aids with spurs and crops because of the physical challenge of riding ten or twenty horses each day. After four or five rides, even the best rider loses a good share of his leg strength.

As with other sports, horsemanship is learned in stages, each skill developed before moving on to the next level. A rider must master position, balance, and proper use of natural aids in order to become what we

The "natural aids" include the legs (which have the primary function of moving the horse forward, backward, or sideways) and the hands (whose primary function is to communicate desired speed and direction). All natural aids are used in combination to achieve all functions.

Equitation involves communication with the horse, often using numerous aids simultaneously to reach your goals. In asking for a stop and roll-back, I'm coordinating leg, rein, seat, and voice aids, while monitoring his response.

call a "quiet rider," one who communicates with the horse without unintentional jiggles and bounces. Once he has perfected his use of natural aids, he can advance to artificial aids.

LEG AIDS

Let's review how leg aids work. Basically, a horse reacts to leg pressure on his side by moving *away* from the pressure. Although a young colt might initially have the opposite reaction—moving *toward* the pressure—he soon learns that the

easiest way to relieve the pressure is to move away from it. This "learned instinct" is one of several predictable responses to stimuli that we can use to train the horse.

Leg aids are either active or inactive. Although both kinds of aids are used to communicate something to the horse, active legs are *moving* the horse in some way, while inactive legs are *holding* the horse in position. Many people think that when riding, you either use your legs or you don't, but actually, you seldom do nothing with your legs. They will either be active or inactive.

A correct leg is relaxed and natural, with a "grip" on the horse. Get a grip by concentrating on two points of contact—just above your knee, and just below. If you handle these spots correctly, the rest of the leg falls into place.

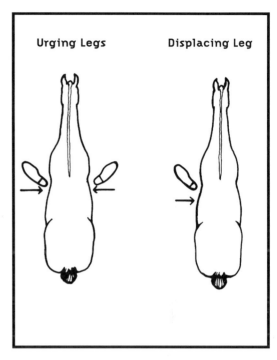

Active Leg Aids

Active Legs

There are two types of active, or moving, aids. The type of leg aids with which you may be most familiar move the horse forward or backward. These "urging legs" are usually used together as a pair, prompting the horse to move faster. An example is the transition to a trot, in which you squeeze with two urging legs to get the desired gait.

Think of using your urging legs the way you use your fingers to squeeze toothpaste from a tube. You squeeze the sides of the horse with both legs to push the desired product—in this case, forward motion—out the front. This visualization is useful when we talk about riding the horse "in front of your leg" (in other words,

being a strong rider with lots of impulsion).

The second type of active aids are "displacing legs," which move the horse laterally from side to side. The displacing leg moves into the horse, and the horse relieves the pressure by moving away from the leg. For example, to ask a horse to sidepass (walk sideways by crossing his feet over each other laterally) to the left, you would cue with a displacing leg on the right side of the horse.

Inactive (Holding) Legs

There is only one type of inactive leg aid, but it is used perhaps more than any other aid. The "holding leg" is similar to the displacing leg, except

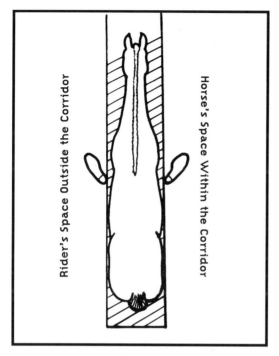

Inactive Leg Aids

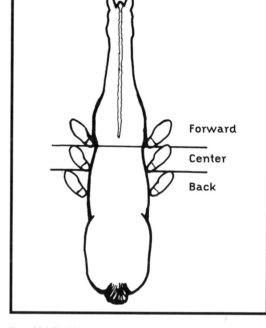

Leg Aid Positions

instead of moving the horse out of a space, it keeps the horse *in* that space. I like to think of the holding leg as a border between the "rider's space" and the "horse's space."

Holding legs are considered inactive because as long as the horse stays within his space, he feels no pressure from the holding leg. But holding legs are also a "responsive" aid; if the horse moves into the rider's space, the holding leg turns into an active displacing leg, pushing the horse back into his own space. In effect, the rider creates a corridor between his legs that is just wide enough for the horse to move through. As long as the horse moves within that corridor, the rider will leave him alone. When the horse begins to push the boundaries of that corridor, he will bump into the rider's holding leg, triggering the displacing leg that will move him back into his corridor of travel.

Leg Positions

Whether you are using active or inactive leg aids, you can affect the horse's response by adjusting the position of your legs. The normal position beneath the body is the center position, sometimes called "at the girth." However, that is a misleading term since your legs actually hang behind the girth. Use of the legs in the center position will affect the entire horse. A typical use of this aid would be the sidepassing example mentioned earlier. To move the entire horse left, the rider would use a displacing leg centered on the right.

Use of legs "forward" of center will tend to affect the front end of the horse more than the rear, while leg aids in the "back" position will affect the rear more than the front. To reach the forward position, you force the heel down a little

The leg aids can be used in three positions to affect the horse in different ways. The "forward position" or "in front of the girth" moves the horse's front end, as in a turn on the haunches.

The "center position," or "at the girth," tends to move the whole body, as in a sidepass or half pass. We typically use urging legs at the center position, where your good equitation legs normally hang.

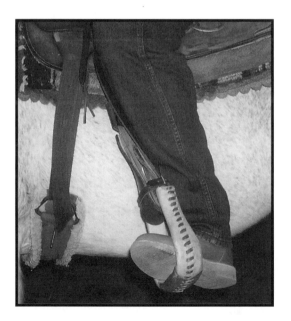

The "back position," or "behind the girth," moves the horse's hindquarters, as in a turn on the forehand, or a canter transition. You reach the back position by lifting the heel a bit and turning the toe slightly.

more than usual. To get to the back position, you lift your heel a bit, turning the toe out slightly. The difference between forward and back positions is only about three or four inches.

You can apply any of the leg aids in different intensities to get different responses from the horse. In increasing order of intensity, you can apply squeezing, tapping, or kicking legs. Using the least severe aids possible to obtain the desired response maintains the invisible communication that is the ideal of equitation. To get a more immediate or extensive response, you can use a more intense aid. In other words, start with the least intense aids, adding more intensity only if you need to.

REIN AIDS

Rein aids are perhaps the most specialized and precise method of communication with your horse. In the days before automobiles, skilled

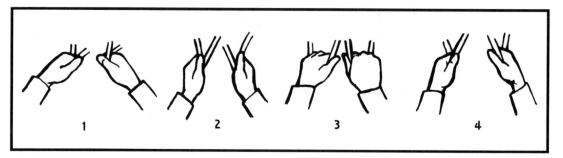

Two-Handed Rein Carriage

1. Incorrect— Thumbs pointed inward, knuckles too close together. I'll bet this person has the elbows sticking out!

2. Incorrect—Thumbs pointed outward, wrist broken. I'll bet this guy is forty years old and still living with his mother.

3. Incorrect—Wrists are straight but palms are turned down. Some people call this "piano hands." I call it "nuns getting ready to whack you on the hands with a ruler" hands.

4. Correct position—Wrists are straight, palms turned down slightly, fingers closed around the reins, thumbs pointing toward the bit

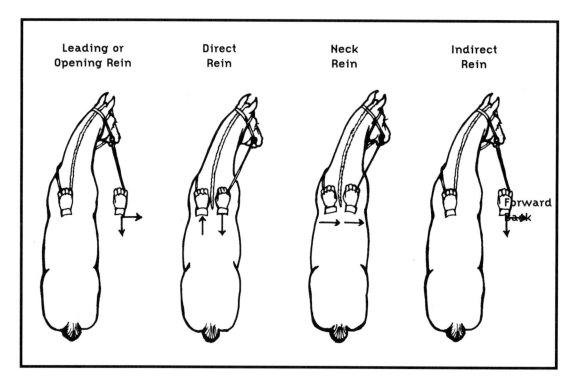

The Rein Aids

reinsmen were highly prized for their talents and could easily find work in any town driving a stage or freight wagon. Rein aids are skills that don't come naturally—they must be developed.

Like leg aids, rein aids employ the learned instinct that controls how the horse reacts to our aids. Once the horse has learned that the easiest way to relieve the pressure of the bit is to bend his head in the direction of the pressure, you can use various rein aids to achieve varying degrees and types of control.

Leading Rein

Sometimes called "opening" rein, the leading rein aid is usually the first that a horse will learn. With the use of a snaffle bit, the rider carries a rein in each hand and pulls one or the other to the side to "lead" the horse's head through the turn. Some colts will at first resist, but soon learn to relieve the discomfort by turning the head where it's being pulled.

Using the leading rein teaches the horse how to give his head to the rider. To turn left, the rider pulls his left rein outward and back, leading the horse's nose to the left. Most horses' early training is spent circling and turning at a trot with a leading rein. Using the leading rein teaches the horse to be relaxed and flexible with his head and neck. In training, I often use a leading rein with an opposite holding leg. While asking the horse to stand still with my holding legs, I turn his head from side to side. This makes him softer and more responsive to my hands.

Direct Rein

The "direct" reining technique (also called "plow reining") is more sophisticated than the leading

Erika demonstrates the "opening rein." Notice how she has also laterally displaced her weight to the left, and has opened her left leg to allow the horse room to turn. Also known as the "leading rein" in western training, this is the most basic of rein aids.

Two-handed rein aids, very useful in western training and schooling, are usually performed with a snaffle, or a broken and hinged western bit like a Tom Thumb or Billy Allen. This rider is demonstrating a "direct rein."

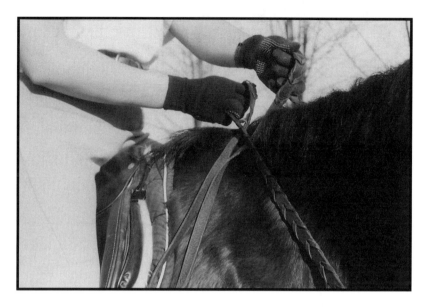

An indirect rein in the *forward* position will direct rein the head and neck to the right while neck reining the shoulder out to the left. This is useful in bending a horse through a turn without letting him fall into the center.

rein aid. This technique provides the most direct contact between the rider's hands and the horse's mouth. The direct rein turns the bit, and the horse is trained to respond to the turning bit. As with leading reins, the rider holds a rein in each hand. If he wants to turn left, he pulls straight back on the left rein, while pushing forward slightly with the right rein, allowing the bit to turn in the horse's mouth.

The direct rein is the primary rein aid for most English riding. In hunt seat or dressage, the horse responds entirely to direct reining. This direct contact with the horse's mouth is consistent with the philosophy behind English-style riding, which emphasizes constant, direct contact with the horse. Direct reining is also the most useful rein aid for training and schooling the Western performance horse. Most Western trainers routinely pick up a two-handed rein carriage with every horse they ride.

Neck Rein

Although "neck reining" is generally considered a Western aid, it has many useful applications in

English riding, and is commonly taught to finished hunter equitation and dressage horses. In English or Western riding, neck reining is a more advanced aid that the horse cannot learn until he is sufficiently responsive to the direct rein.

The neck rein is based on a training concept completely different than leading or direct reining. Properly executed, the neck rein doesn't even contact the bit; instead, we train the horse to move away from rein pressure on his *neck*. The neck reining technique developed out of necessity because it provided for the needs of the nineteenth-century Mexican and American cowboys: carrying both reins in one hand allowed them to rope or shoot with the other hand. More important, the minimal contact kept the horse's mouth fresh during the routine ten-hour rides.

Although most Western riders today don't rope or shoot with their free hand, horses and riders are not considered "finished" until they learn to neck rein properly. In the reining class, which is generally considered the most advanced stage of Western riding, the horse performs difficult changes of speed, direction, and lead—all executed with a one-handed neck rein. However they school, Western showhorses are normally expected to be ridden one-handed except in snaffle bit pleasure classes, in which two- or three-year-olds are shown in a snaffle or bosal.

A rider can execute a neck rein from either hand (traditionally, cowboys held the reins in the weaker hand), holding the reins centered over the withers, just in front of or above the saddle horn. This position allows unrestricted but precise hand movement. The reins typically lie over the index finger, with that finger between the reins. Held in this way, the reins can be shortened or lengthened while riding. To turn the horse's head to the left, the rider *lifts* his hand to the left, keeping the fingers closed and the wrist straight. This motion automatically causes the left rein to slacken and at the same time lays the right rein across the right side of the horse's neck.

Indirect Rein

For both horse and rider, the most complicated of the rein aids is the "indirect" rein, a combination of direct and neck reins. It asks the horse to do conflicting movements with his head and shoulder.

From a two-handed rein carriage, an indirect rein to the left starts just like a direct rein. Then, while pulling the rein back with the left hand, the rider angles that hand inward over the horse's withers, direct reining to the left while simultaneously neck reining to the right.

Although hunter riders often tell me that their horses can't neck rein but respond to indirect reining, a horse must be responding to both direct *and* neck reins (at least a little) before he can understand indirect reining. Therefore, horses that understand indirect reining should easily learn neck reining.

The indirect rein is used very sparingly, reserved mostly for advanced schooling situations. For example, an indirect rein could be used with a horse that wants to drift toward the center of an arena. The rider can probably move the horse away from the center with a neck rein or an outside direct rein, usually in combination with an inside displacing leg. But those rein aids won't let him accurately steer around the turn, or bend the horse on an inside arc to the circle.

Used with a right holding leg, an indirect rein in the back position (or "behind the horn") will also twist the hip to the outside. This is the most severe of the rein aids and should not be overused.

Perfect hands at the canter are straight from elbow to bit, with fingers closed and relaxed, making good contact with the horse. I teach riders to have "elastic arms," stretching and retracting automatically so they're riding with "broomstick" reins that are always straight.

The solution is the indirect rein, which turns the head and neck inside, while holding the shoulder outside.

There are two types of indirect reins, depending on the position of the hands during execution. Indirect reins are either "forward" or "back" (or, in Western riding, "in front of" or "behind" the saddle horn). I have already explained the indirect rein forward. The indirect rein *behind* the saddle horn is used in precisely the same way, but since the hand is further back (above the pommel of the saddle) it has a slightly different effect on the horse; it will twist the horse's balance on an axis over the front feet. While turning the head one direction, this aid will neck rein the shoulder in the opposite direction, twisting the horse's hip in the same direction as his shoulder.

Suppose you have a horse that canters with his hip carried inside the circle. You could try to push his hip out with your displacing leg, but that might make him "bulge" to the outside of the circle. You could also try to direct rein the front end to the inside while displacing the hip to the outside with your leg.

As a result, the horse may spiral inside to the unsupported shoulder. The solution? The indirect rein in the "back" position will direct rein the head on the arc of the circle while neck reining the shoulder out and helping to twist the hip out.

Supporting Rein

The "supporting" rein is often used with an opposite active rein aid (in a two-handed rein carriage) to control the intensity of the active rein. For example, let's say you are executing a circle to the left. You use your direct rein to set the horse's head on the arc of the circle, but he overflexes to the inside. Although he is moving through the circle nicely, not challenging your inside bending leg, his head and neck are bent too far inside. What should you do? Use a supporting rein on the outside to regulate the effect of the inside direct rein. In other words, direct rein to the left with your left hand, while straightening out the horse's head and neck with your right hand.

"Mr. Crotchrider" is sitting off his seat bone too much, perching on the front of his saddle. While he is demonstrating a western saddle, these hip angle concepts apply to any discipline.

SEAT AND WEIGHT AIDS

Many riders underestimate the effectiveness of seat and weight aids. I often speak of the seat and weight interchangeably, which is loosely correct. The seat is the primary instrument for using weight aids, but a horse will respond to variations in weight distribution that are as slight as a turn of the head. A horse will adjust his own carriage to adapt to the weight distribution of the rider. To put it simply, a horse will drift in the direction you are leaning in an effort to stay beneath you. This learned instinct is based on the relationship between the centers of balance of the horse and rider.

A horse's center of balance is that point at which his weight is distributed evenly from front to back and from side to side. His build will affect his center of balance; for example, a horse with a short neck and heavy rear end will have a center of balance slightly behind average (the same can be said for some people!). A horse with light hindquarters and an extraordinarily long neck would tend to be very heavy on the forehand.

The rider's center of balance is located directly in front of his seat bones, and is therefore slightly behind that of the horse. If the horse's and rider's centers of balance lined up vertically, it would be much easier for the horse to carry a rider. Think about how it feels to carry a child in your arms. The child gets heavy quickly because you are carrying him to the side of your center. However, when sitting on your shoulders—stacking the centers of balance one above the other—he becomes much easier to carry.

Watch a two-year-old colt in early training. He carries an empty saddle easily (even though he might not like it) because the saddle's center of balance is approximately over his own. Then put a person in the saddle and watch what happens: the horse struggles to maintain his balance. He has trouble turning and making his transitions because he is trying to adjust to the weight on his back. A good rider can make adjustments to a horse's way of going that will affect the horse's center of balance. The rider uses weight aids to facilitate the horse's movements and to compensate for the difference between his own center of balance and the horse's.

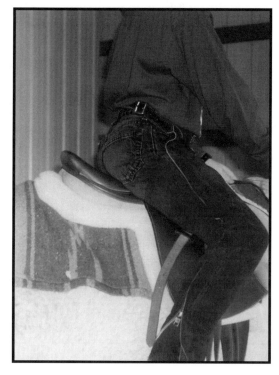

"Mister Mustachio" shows a nice, relaxed leg, riding on the inside of the thigh, with contact just
below the knee. Don't wrap your leg around the
barrel—your feet should be at least as wide as your
knees. You don't have to be "bowlegged" to ride
western, just really relaxed.

Seat and weight aids are used actively or passively
to alter the relationship between the horse's and
rider's centers of balance. Shifting forward or
back between seat bones and crotch is "vertical"
displacement, while shifting side to side from one
seat bone to the other is "lateral" displacement.

The vertical lines repre-
sent the horse's center
of balance in motion (H)
and the rider's center of
balance (R). The horse
becomes accustomed to
carrying this differen-
tial and responds to any
deviation.

Seat Position

Because the seat is the primary weight aid, its position is important. The rider should sit in the center of the saddle, in the lowest part—not propped on the cantle, or straddling the pommel. The rider's seat should balance on three points of contact: the crotch and the two seat bones, with all three points carrying equal weight. The rider's lower back should be flat and relaxed, not arched or rounded. The thighs should hang down the horse's sides, without pinching together or sliding forward.

The relationship between the legs and the upper body determines the "hip angle," or angle of the pelvis. The best indication of hip angle is the seam on the side of your jeans or breeches, which we normally want to line up vertically. If the seam is angled forward of vertical, you are "perching" on the pommel. If it is angled behind vertical, you are "sitting on your pockets." In both cases, hip angle is wrong.

Vertical Weight Displacement

Vertical weight displacement, the first basic weight aid, occurs when the rider leans or shifts his hip angle forward or backward along the axis of the horse. For example, if the rider leans forward slightly onto his crotch, he closes the gap between his own center of balance and that of the horse. The horse reacts to the change by trying to shift the rider's center back to the original position; he speeds up, trying to "move up under" the rider.

You might want to use this aid on a horse that plods along, dragging his feet, with no energy or impulse. (You can use your legs, but a horse like that can wear you out in a hurry!) By shifting hip angle forward and sitting heavily on the crotch, you urge the horse to increase speed—sort of the reverse of the half-halt. Hunt riders can post from the forward position, "dragging" the horse forward by closing the distance between centers even more on every post. A hip angle that is constantly more forward than stock seat or dressage seat is part of what makes hunter seat the "forward seat." The fundamental concept of forward seat is an upper body position that centers the rider more closely to the center of balance of the horse.

The opposite aid is vertical weight displacement back, in which the rider opens the hip angle, sitting heavier on his seat bones. This movement shifts the rider's center of balance back slightly, and the horse responds by "dropping back under" the rider, again trying to maintain the relationship between his own center of balance and that of the rider. The horse slows pace to let the rider catch up.

A hunt rider posting "behind the motion" is using the vertical weight displacement technique to quiet a high-strung, very fast horse. The rider shifts hip angle back, posting from a very flat seat, with less height and more vertically than a forward seat rider would. Consequently, the horse drops back under the rider and moves at a more relaxed pace.

Hip angle, leg position, and upper body position must all coordinate to form correct posture. An error in one often causes error in another. For example, a rider sitting on his pockets, with hip angle behind vertical, is forcing the hip joints forward. That makes the legs hang too far forward, so upper body balance also falls behind vertical. If the hips are tilted *forward* of the vertical, the lower back will arch, and the upper back and shoulders will tend to be carried too far forward.

Above: The rider is sitting behind the motion at the "hip open" position of the canter, perhaps in an attempt to slow and quiet a fiery horse.

Right: The forward postion of the posting trot, on the left diagonal. Notice the upper body angle. I want hunter riders at about a fifteen degree angle at the posting trot, and at the canter, to stay with the forward motion of the horse. Of course, this is followed by . . .

. . . the back position of the posting trot, one step later. Start thinking of your posting motion as forward and back rather than up and down. It will help to keep your center of gravity close to the horse as you post, to keep you from being top heavy.

Below: Compare the back position of the posting trot to this example of the sitting trot. Can you see that you never really sit in your posting. Even in the sitting trot you are a couple of degrees in front of the vertical.

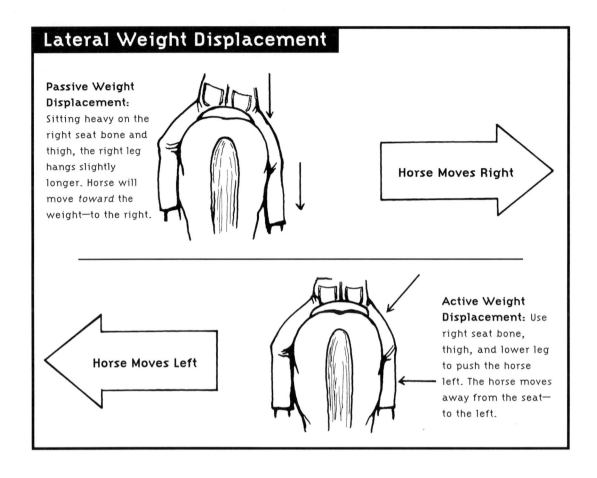

Lateral Weight Displacement

Passive Weight Displacement: Sitting heavy on the right seat bone and thigh, the right leg hangs slightly longer. Horse will move *toward* the weight—to the right.

Horse Moves Right

Horse Moves Left

Active Weight Displacement: Use right seat bone, thigh, and lower leg to push the horse left. The horse moves away from the seat—to the left.

Lateral Weight Displacement

The second basic weight aid is lateral weight displacement. As with vertical weight displacement, the horse is accustomed to the relationship between his own center of balance and that of the rider, and responds to shifts in weight by moving to align his own center underneath the rider's.

To accomplish lateral weight displacement, the rider shifts his weight onto one seat bone, allowing the thigh on the same side to hang more heavily. (A rider who becomes too aggressive with lateral weight displacement can reverse the effect, asking the horse to move in the opposite direction.) The weight shift that draws the horse's center beneath the rider's center creates a "passive"

weight displacement. An "active" weight displacement involves displacement with the seat and legs combined with a passive weight displacement in the same direction.

Suppose you are watching a super-slow-motion video of a rider asking a horse for a flying lead change from right to left. The rider starts with basic lateral weight displacement to the right. He shifts to a displacing right seat, thigh, and calf. As the horse shifts weight to change leads, the rider shifts lateral weight displacement to the left while releasing with his left leg.

Using lateral weight displacement is sort of like using a mouse on your computer: you press and drag to move files from one place to another.

Likewise, as my horse crosses the center of a figure-eight, I press and drag my saddle from one circle to another using active lateral weight displacement. Lateral weight displacement is most commonly used to execute specialized lateral movements, such as sidepasses and turns on the haunches or forehand. It is also used in figure work, to keep a line straight, or to support a round circle.

VOICE AIDS

Although the effectiveness of voice aids cannot be seriously questioned, the extent of their usefulness is somewhat limited. The voice is used primarily as an active aid during early training, starting with ground work. Ideally, the horse will be carrying a saddle and working at all gaits on a longe line before the rider ever tries to mount him. With the aid of a longe whip, he should be taught to execute each gait and halt

We teach beginners to ask a horse for a canter lead by pushing the horse's shoulder outside with the hands and kicking with the outside leg. Better riders can help balance the horse thorugh the transition.

upon voice command, and should be drilled on transitions and familiarity with the vocal cues.

As the horse becomes familiar with the cue-response scenario, the trainer begins to use the more permanent aids. During this transition, the trainer uses the voice first and follows with the corresponding leg and rein aids. Eventually, the horse learns to respond to the leg and rein aids, and the voice becomes a passive aid. Soon the voice aid can be discontinued entirely.

Voice aids are especially helpful to inexperienced riders, who typically are very ineffective in their use of natural aids. Often these riders are unsure of proper usage or lack the muscular coordination to use the legs or reins exactly as they know they should. This is why I teach beginners on very quiet, experienced horses that understand simple voice aids. Usually the beginning rider's voice can communicate with the horse better than his other natural aids.

All horses appreciate praise when they have done well, or a soothing voice when they're frightened or excited. A scolding probably does more than anything else to discipline a horse when he has intentionally done wrong. Horses seem to understand tone of voice; your words aren't as important as the way you say them. When used to calm or to reward behavior, the voice is a passive aid. It is not an active or primary aid in these instances because it isn't part of the cue-response scenario.

As a passive aid, the voice is useful for everyday interaction with horses of any age. While a weanling colt hasn't the first clue about cue-response scenarios, he will respond to a calm voice when it comes time to deworm or give shots. A yearling understands the angry voice when he rears up as you are trying to lead him. A mare giving birth will appreciate a reassuring word of encouragement. The passive voice is the one natural aid that has universal and lifelong application in the interaction between human and horse.

 CHAPTER FIVE

USING ARTIFICIAL AIDS

After reading about the use of natural aids in training, you're probably wondering how your favorite old spurs fit into the picture. Spurs fall under the category of "artificial aids," which include pretty much anything other than a natural aid that you might use to train the horse. Artificial aids can benefit an experienced horseman; the trick is knowing how to use them. I often have to tell my students that a crop is for making the horse go, not for beating him after he stops!

As an instructor, I discourage extensive use of artificial aids. Over the years, I've had to retrain dozens of freshmen in the proper use of leg aids, because they grew up completely dependent on unneeded spurs.

I like to think of artificial aids as tools that are used to make a job easier. Take a calculator, for instance. Once you understand how to solve a math problem, a calculator merely helps you arrive at the solution faster. It is not a substitute for understanding. When I was in school, I learned calculus first, before I was allowed to use a calculator. This is how it should be when you are learning to ride: You should be sure you comprehend equitation concepts before using artificial aids.

SPURS

Most everyone seems to like spurs—it's as though they make you feel invincible or something. I know people who have spurs who don't even ride! They just like the look of them, keep them lying around the house as decoration. Pick up a catalog from any major tack supplier and you'll find more varieties of spurs and crops than riding helmets. What does this say to us?!

Used correctly in the proper situations, spurs can be one of the most valuable tools for a trainer. Riding is a physically demanding sport, and a

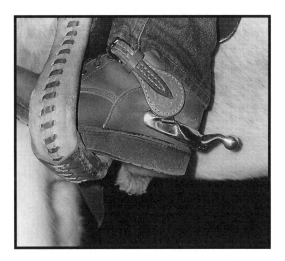

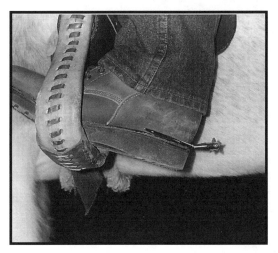

These are my favorite "marble spurs," with a lit- tle ball where the rowel would be. They give you a little extra zing in your leg, but you can't pos- sibly cut a horse even if you mess up. They come in all variations, both English and Western.

As an equitation trainer, I'm not a big advocate of spurs. However, they are useful for small children without much leverage in their legs or for adults who ride a lot of horses. This slip-on "pizza cutter" spur is easy to get on and off during a lesson.

trainer who rides many horses each day is extremely appreciative of the energy savings that spurs provide. Spurs are particularly useful for reschooling a horse, often an older animal, that is simply locking up and doesn't want to go for- ward. You know the type. You can kick for all you're worth and it still wears you out to ride once around the ring. I have an old lesson horse that my daughter renamed "Cow." (I know you're smiling because everybody knows a horse like this.) I'm not trying to make excuses for Cow, but an older horse is often dead-sided. I mean that literally. The nerves in his sides can become desensitized to the rider's leg, so it really isn't much trouble for him to just ignore your leg entirely. A little reschooling with some blunt spurs will usually have a drastic and perhaps long-lasting effect.

When you do use spurs, the universal rule of training applies: You should use the least severe aid first, then progress to something more severe if needed. A professional rider uses spurs so seldom

and so subtly that it's hard to notice when he does. Start by using your leg, keeping the spur off the horse. If he doesn't respond to your leg, follow up immediately and firmly with the spur to reinforce your cue (although not so firmly as to spur yourself out of the saddle!). Eventually the horse will learn that if he responds to the leg, he won't have to deal with the spur.

It should be obvious that you need to use spurs responsibly. If you ever see the effects of improperly used spurs, it will teach you a lesson you will never forget. A few years ago, I agreed to train a horse that had come from such an experience. The first-time owner had paid a man to tune up an older quarter horse gelding she had recently purchased. But when she checked on her horse after six weeks, she was told he still was not safe for her to ride. The woman came to me with reports of open wounds and purple bruises on the sides of her palomino horse, wanting to know if they were the result of stan- dard training practice!

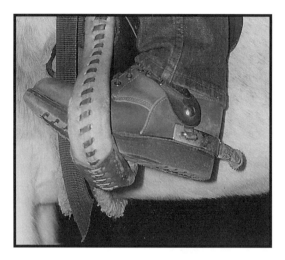

A variation of this basic "cutting spur" is used by probably eighty percent of all the quarter horse owners in the world! Some show spurs can be very elaborate and expensive, with fancy tooled leather and precious metals and gems!

Some variation of this blunt English spur is commonly used for hunters, jumpers, eventers, and even polo (but not water polo!).

I kept the horse in a stall for several days before I even tried to touch him. He would swing his butt to the door and kick with both barrels whenever someone walked past the stall. After about a week, I could ride the horse enough to find out that I couldn't put a leg anywhere near him. Big surprise! I backed off and went to ground work, teaching him voice commands and gait stability while working him in a round pen. After a couple of weeks on the ground, he was responding well to voice, and his sides were healed enough that I rode him for another couple of weeks in the round pen, using only voice aids. Six weeks later, I was able to gradually bring my leg back onto the horse. Now his owner can ride him bareback on trails, and she actually uses spurs for jumping. He is as gentle and quiet a horse as you will find anywhere.

If I had to recommend a pair of spurs for general use, I wouldn't hesitate to name what I call "marble" spurs—those with the marble-sized round ball on the end. They come in many styles, from hunter-style marble nubs to dressage shanks with marbles and Western "cutting"-style spurs with marble tips. This blunt tip is plenty of spur for most horses and especially for most riders. The only bad thing about marble spurs is that they don't make that cool "ching-ching-ching" sound when you walk around!

CROPS AND WHIPS

A crop is a versatile artificial aid, usually used to move or collect a lazy horse. However, I've seen it used for many other purposes, including getting a cat out of a tree. I once saw a woman in the tack room taping a thumb tack to the end of her crop, and I almost had a stroke! She used it to scratch her back. Seriously, though, I often give a crop to students I would never trust with spurs. Crops are easier to learn to use than spurs, and much less destructive to the

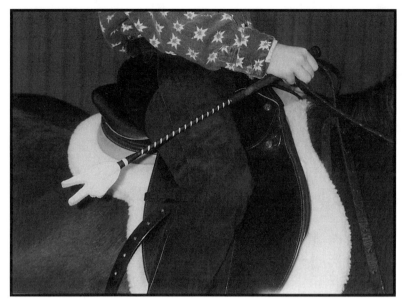

This rider is demonstrating the proper way to hold a crop. An inch or so of knob extends beyond the top of her hand, fingers closed naturally around the reins. The crop should be carried against the thigh, not held so that it flaps around the horse. (I might choose a more conservative crop than this one for a show!)

training process if used incorrectly. If you screw up, it's easy to drop a crop and ride away.

I teach hunter equitation riders to carry a crop in the outside hand and to change hands when changing directions in the ring. Think about it. You use the crop to assist your leg, right? The canter is the hardest gait for a lazy horse, and you cue for the canter with an active outside leg. So doesn't it make sense that you will most likely need your crop to aid your outside leg when cueing for the canter?

You should hold the crop an inch or so below the knob, letting it lie flat against or above your knee. If you get into the habit of carrying it that way, you won't have to worry about inadvertently touching the shoulder of a horse that is particularly shy of the crop.

When using the crop to aid your leg, you should tap the horse just behind your leg. Many riders have the bad habit of reaching back to the hindquarters to urge the horse forward. Although this technique works, it fails to teach the horse to associate the urging leg with the urging crop. Others have the worse habit of flicking the crop

against the horse's shoulder without even taking the hand off the reins. If you have the proper rein contact, using a crop this way will be difficult without pulling on the horse's mouth and accidentally giving him mixed signals.

Using a crop on the shoulder is sending the horse mixed signals in another way. Suppose you squeeze with your urging legs, and your horse moves forward away from the pressure. When you smack a crop against his shoulder, his training tells him to back off from *that* aid as well. In effect, you are impeding his forward motion with the very aid you are using to urge him on.

Dressage riders typically use a very long whip (at least, it's long compared to the short jumping crops hunter equitation riders carry). Dressage is a discipline that emphasizes the constant and ongoing training of the horse; therefore, dressage whips are more functional for moving the shoulder or hip laterally than for achieving forward impulsion. Dressage riders generally carry the whip to the inside, changing hands as they reverse direction. This is perhaps because the primary concern of those trainers is to keep the horse tracking on the

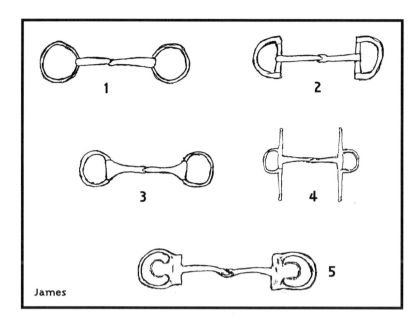

Examples of Common Snaffle Bits

1. O-Ring Snaffle
2. Dee-Ring Snaffle
3. Egg-Butt Snaffle
4. Full Cheek Snaffle
5. Western Show Snaffle

James

line. Most horses tend to carry the hips slightly inside, so the dressage whip is designed to deal with this tendency and situations like it.

My preference for general pleasure riding is a twenty-inch crop with a small "popper," so called because of the sound made by the folded leather loop on the end when you smack the horse. The horse responds mostly because he is afraid of the popping sound, so you don't have to strike him very hard. I hate a wristband that prevents you from dropping the crop because when you inevitably *do* lose the crop, it is still attached to your hand and flops around out of control, banging against the horse randomly. I much prefer a crop that will drop to the ground if you lose your grip. It seems to me that if you have trouble holding your crop, you don't really need a handy wrist band—you need more practice holding your crop.

LEVERAGE DEVICES

"Artificial leverage" sounds like something from a corporate takeover story on the front page of the *Wall Street Journal*. Actually, leverage devices include anything that gives the rider increased pressure on the bit or the horse's poll, changes the angle or effect of the pressure on the bit, or both. We usually use leverage devices to correct a horse that evades the bit by getting above it or braces against the bit when you pull on the reins.

Curb Bits

Curb bits are more severe than snaffles and provide the simplest example of leverage on the horse's mouth. Because you ride without contact when neck reining, this type of reining requires a more severe bit to maintain collection and proper head carriage. Although most people think you should use a more severe bit on a rogue that needs discipline, the opposite is true. The less trained a horse is, the more control is needed; therefore, the less severe the bit must be to maintain a fresh mouth. Conversely, the more finished a horse is, the more subtle the aids can be; consequently, a more severe bit must be used to detect subtle aids.

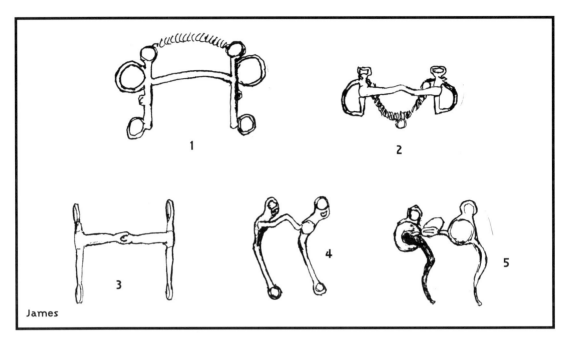

James

Examples of Common Curb Bits

1. Pelham (usually used with double reins)
2. Kimberwicke (with adjustable rein slots)
3. Tom Thumb "Snaffle" (really a curb)

4. Common Western Grazing Bit
5. Half-Spade (close variation: "correction" bit)

Curb bits come in a variety of styles, but the common denominator is that they have the reins attached to shanks, and they have a curb chain. As the reins are drawn, the mouthpiece is pulled tightly down against the bars of the mouth. The bit rotates, pulling the curb chain or strap up against the "curb area" of the bars of the jaw. The shanks pull the mouthpiece down onto the mouth, while the curb chain is drawn up under the chin, trapping the jawbone between. At the same time, the bridle is drawn down, putting pressure on the poll. The only way for the horse to relieve the pressure is to rotate with the bit, breaking at the poll and tucking his nose in and down. These "correction" bits are typically for well-trained horses that won't pay attention without a lot of bit.

The Western bits we use on our school horses are called "Tom Thumb" bits. They are the least severe of all curb bits because they have a broken mouthpiece and a hinged joint attached to a short shank. Most people think that a jointed bit is always a snaffle, when in fact it's the action of a bit that makes it a snaffle or a curb. The Tom Thumb bit is ideal for teaching because it dissipates most unintentional movement of the reins and prevents bouncy hands from causing major confusion for the horse. However, you shouldn't expect much precision control from the Tom Thumb because the pressure of the reins is absorbed by all the jointed, moving parts, and the horse doesn't feel it.

Draw Reins

Rather than having to change the bit, trainers often use draw reins to change the way a horse carries a

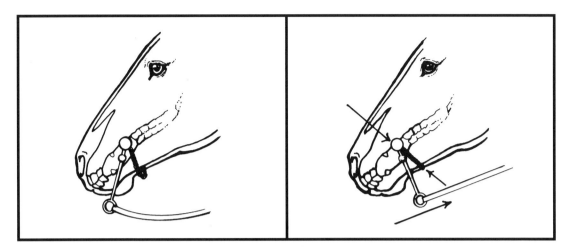

The Curb Action

The bit lying relaxed in the horse's mouth is carried mostly on the tongue, one of the least sensitive of the pressure points. The curb chain is relaxed.

As the reins are drawn, the leverage of the curb action draws the curb chain up onto the bars of the jaw, while the mouthpiece is drawn down onto the bars of the mouth. These are the two most sensitive pressure points.

bit. In this leverage technique, a long set of reins runs from the center of the girth, through the rings of the snaffle, then back to the rider. Since the reins slide freely through the bit, your pull on the reins draws the horse's head down and toward his chest. The harder you pull, the lower and tighter his head carriage will be. If the horse pulls back, he is jerking mostly against the anchored end of the reins, so it's much easier for you to handle the bit. This arrangement can be compared to a pulley system, with the bit being the movable pulley at the center of your rope. Draw reins are most commonly used to train hunt seat horses with a snaffle bit, or with a big-ring Western training snaffle. They are never allowed in competition.

Running Martingales

A running martingale, or "training fork," is based on the same principle as draw reins. The martin-gale attachment is anchored to the center of the girth, and the reins run through the rings of the fork to the rider. As the reins are pulled, the horse's head is pulled down and in. The running martingale does not restrict the horse's natural head movements as much as draw reins do. Therefore, trainers commonly use it for Western horses that need to be ridden with less contact. Running martingales are also popular for training jumping horses because jumping requires collected control of the horse's head without restricting the natural balancing motions of his head and neck.

Fixed Aids

Sometimes a horse will tend to carry his head high, not necessarily trying to evade the bit, but just as a general way of going. This kind of carriage can often be attributed to conformation if the neck is

Leverage Factor

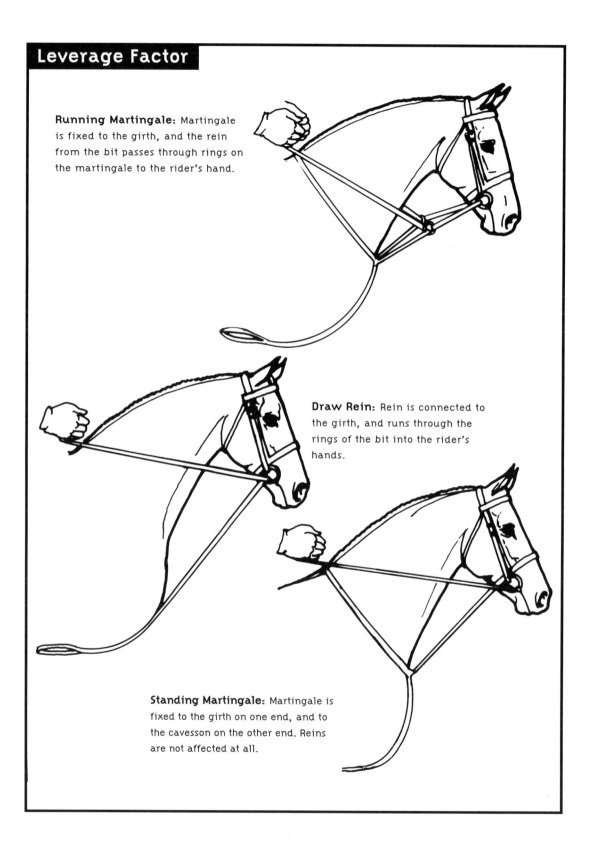

Running Martingale: Martingale is fixed to the girth, and the rein from the bit passes through rings on the martingale to the rider's hand.

Draw Rein: Rein is connected to the girth, and runs through the rings of the bit into the rider's hands.

Standing Martingale: Martingale is fixed to the girth on one end, and to the cavesson on the other end. Reins are not affected at all.

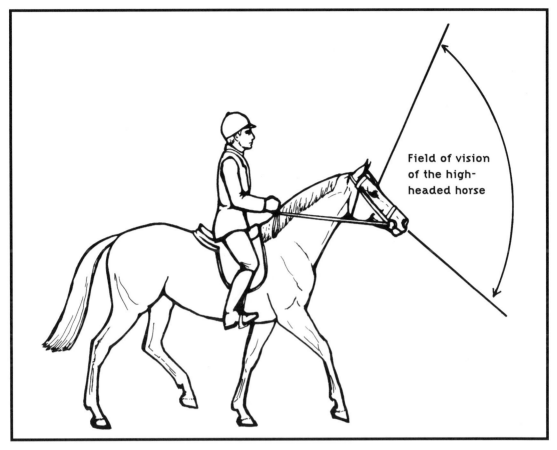

Field of vision of the high-headed horse

A high-headed horse may not be able to see the ground in front of his line of movement. A pretty good reason to use a martingale! While he may be perfectly safe to jump, I wouldn't lie down and let him jump me.

set very high into the shoulder, or if the horse is ewe necked. Since the horse moves with better balance and more athleticism with his head and neck arched in a reasonably low position, high-headedness is a disadvantage and will often be corrected by use of fixed aids. Instead of having movable parts like a running martingale or draw reins, fixed aids have both aids affixed to something solid. These include devices such as the "standing martingale" and "tie-down." Fixed aids are not intended to be a training device. Fixed aids simply control an inherently bad situation while they are attached.

One of these fixed aids, the standing martingale, is anchored to the center of the girth, with the other end connected to the cavesson. If the horse raises his head to the set limits of the martingale, he will be restricted by the noseband. It's as simple as that.

The Western equivalent to the standing martingale is known simply as a tie-down. Because Western bridles normally don't have a cavesson, trainers will often add a separate noseband, which I have seen made of anything from leather, to wire cable, to bicycle chain! The typical tie-down outfit sold at tack stores

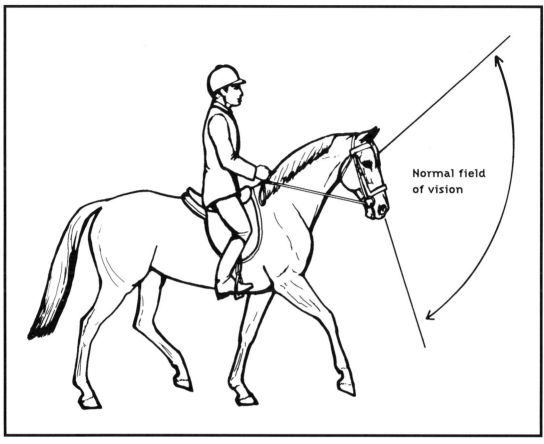

A balanced horse with normal head carriage will have monocular vision at close distance, and binocular vision from afar. In other words, he can see the ground before he steps on it, but does not have good depth perception.

consists of a rubber-covered, wire cable bosal with a nylon strap attached to each end by a spring-loaded snap.

Side Reins

Another variation is the use of "side reins" or "tying around." Mechanically, we could put either into the category of fixed aids, except that the horse does learn and improve through their use, partially as a result of physical development of muscle flexibility and tone. Because they have

no clear-cut category, I call them a variation of fixed aids.

Side reins are used almost identically to draw reins, except that the reins are anchored to the sides of the saddle. They attach either to the ends of the girth or to the D-rings on the western saddle, and pass alongside the horse's shoulders. This provides lateral leverage. The side rein is used mostly for training horses that are very stiff through the shoulders and neck, or horses that won't bend the neck and poll to follow the bit.

Don't confuse these with what hunt seat and dressage people know as "side reins," in which a rein or special side rein attachment is fixed solidly from the bit to the side of the saddle. This type of side rein pulls the horse constantly into a bending position, or holds the neck in a particular headset. They are usually used while longeing, to stretch the neck muscles and make the horse flex to a direction in which he is stiff.

Western trainers use a similar practice they call "tying the horse around." One rein is attached to the D-ring of the saddle to sharply bend the neck into a stiff direction. This is used in the stall or the arena to make the horse more flexible and subservient. I've known western pleasure trainers to leave a horse like that for hours, walking around and around in circles.

Note: When western trainers tie both reins to the D-ring like English side-reins, they normally call that a "bitting rig" of some sort. They longe or ride in bitting rigs to teach the horse flexion of the poll and neck, and to achieve a more dramatic headset. Such rigs are never used in competition.

Bitting Rigs

Head-setting devices, or "bitting rigs," are any combination of bits and external leverage devices that force the horse to carry his head and neck in a certain position. As opposed to martingales or draw reins, bitting rigs are usually homemade, customized to a particular horse and based on the theories of artificial leverage. Head-setting rigs can be used while the horse is being ridden, or they can be designed to work in the stall. Some trainers use bitting rigs while the horse is

turned out loose in the arena or round pen. Although these techniques tend to be more popular among Western riders (since they are generally more concerned about getting the horse's head down), some English practices fall into this category as well, including longeing the horse with side reins.

Technically, anything you could possibly dream up to help train your horse could be classified as an artificial aid (provided it's not a natural aid). The hobbles that American standardbred trainers use to train pacers are artificial aids, as are the weights and chains that trainers use on the hooves of walking horses. Some trainers make their own "war gear" to deal with a particular problem of a particular horse—a good example of mental equitation. Faced with a problem and limited war gear, a good rider will devise his own solution!

A WORD OF WARNING

While a thorough discussion of artificial aids is important to your understanding of mental equitation, I should stress again that artificial aids are intended to *enhance* the natural aids, not to *replace* them. All artificial aids should be used as sparingly as possible, and with the appropriate caution. Keep focused on the natural aids that have worked for centuries, and look cynically upon artificial aids that propose quick (but likely temporary) results. Long-lasting success always comes from study, patience, and sound classical horsemanship.

PERFECTING THE FUNDAMENTALS

The human tendency to rush things causes the most common problems that instructors have with riders, and that trainers have with horses. Because riders often try to go from the beginner stage directly to the advanced stage, many of them (and their horses) never master the critical fundamental skills of the intermediate stage.

Mental equitation provides a clear understanding of what each building block means to the training of horse and rider. With an understanding of these elements of success, students are able to see the "big picture" and the long-term benefits of meticulous hard work. With this insight, they have the discipline to develop a plan and stick to it.

I get new "advanced" students every year who have the basic skills and enthusiasm to develop into exceptional riders. Yet it takes most of them a year or two of polish and maturation to be capable of "finishing" the horse—positively affecting the way he balances and moves. Finishing can include more advanced concepts like collection, correct transitions, or lateral and longitudinal agility. A horse must be well-schooled in fundamentals before the rider can teach him the finishing skills.

How do you know when you and your horse are ready to go on to finishing? At the very least, the horse must know the proper response to all the common uses of the natural aids; he must understand the language we use to request certain movement. More specifically, before the horse is ready to be finished, he must be accomplished in three prerequisites: stabilization, "going on the line," and impulsion.

Western Pleasure class is perhaps the most obvious test of "stabilization"—the horse's ability to maintain pace without contact. The rider "throws the reins away" to show the judge there is no contact. Unfortunately and inaccurately, this has become the western stereotype.

STABILIZATION

Stabilization is the ability of the horse to maintain a consistent pace and stride until he is asked to change them. The concept of stabilization is sort of like "cruise control." You've probably ridden a horse that speeds up, slows down, speeds up, and slows down, over and over. Or maybe he lengthens stride, then shortens it, then lengthens it again. Such a horse is not stabilized or ready for more advanced training. This is because the aids we later use to teach longitudinal agility are the same aids we use to achieve stabilization. You can understand how incredibly confusing it would be for the horse to learn two separate and different concepts simultaneously—for which we use identical aids!

The only way to teach stabilization is through constant monitoring, correction, and—most important—repetition. Once the rider sets the pace, he uses "holding" aids to keep the horse moving at that speed. If the horse doesn't change his pace, he feels no additional aids from the rider. If the horse *does* change pace, the rider corrects him with natural aids. Remember that the horse's reward for a proper response is the discontinuation of the aids. Eventually, the horse learns that regulating his own pace prevents uncomfortable corrections from the rider.

Stabilization is not obvious in the hunter horse because the rider constantly uses natural aids. The real test of stabilization is to use a loose rein, as with a Western horse (see page 68). Since the Western horse is ridden without contact, it is easier to see whether the horse is learning to stabilize himself. If he isn't, it can be easier to teach and maintain stabilization in hunter tack.

There is simply no other way to teach stabilization than through repetition and active use of aids, including a lot of contact with the bit. Because the curb bit is too severe (and the constant

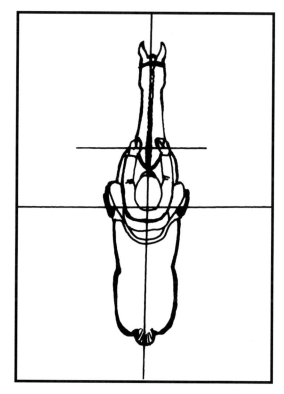

On the Line: The horse is "on the line," with his head in front of him. The rider is sitting squarely with the shoulders, seat, and hands.

contact can damage the mouth), even Western trainers typically use snaffles or hackamores until their horses have accomplished stabilization and are ready to be finished.

GOING ON THE LINE

The second prerequisite to developing finishing skills is the ability of the horse to go "on the line." A horse is moving on the line when his head and neck are bent on the line of passage, his front feet are directly following the head, and his hind feet are following the front feet. For example, when the horse is moving in a straight line, his head must be directly in front of him. In a

Moving toward us "on the line." The rider has the horse balanced up on the vertical; his head leads the way, with the front legs following the head, and the rear legs following the front.

Executing a proper straight line, balanced over both stirrups and both seat bones, with shoulders square and head up. The rider is holding the horse within his space, riding him between holding legs and between the reins.

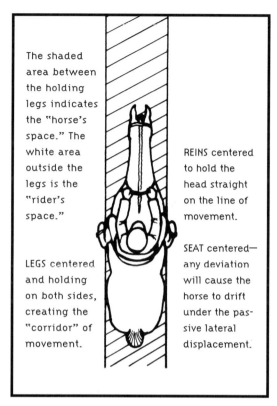

The shaded area between the holding legs indicates the "horse's space." The white area outside the legs is the "rider's space."

LEGS centered and holding on both sides, creating the "corridor" of movement.

REINS centered to hold the head straight on the line of movement.

SEAT centered— any deviation will cause the horse to drift under the passive lateral displacement.

Executing a Straight Line.

turn, the horse's head must be bent on the arc of the curve. A horse that is on the line is more likely to be balanced and agile, and therefore more able to respond to methods for developing longitudinal and lateral agility.

Maybe you're familiar with the concept of "tracking," in which the horse's rear feet fall in the tracks of the front feet as he moves. This is similar to being on the line, but not quite the same. In putting the horse on the line, we're more concerned with body alignment than foot placement. Some horses track with their feet but "rubber neck" the head and neck in the opposite direction. If any of the horse's three assemblies—

the head and neck, forehand, and hindquarters— are off the line of passage, the horse is not on the line. The line of passage can be a straight line or part of a circle. Of course, the arc of the turn and the line of passage will be different for a small circle than for a large one. Therefore, the horse's head and neck must bend differently for different size circles.

I seldom ride around the rail when I am schooling a horse. The key to keeping the horse's attention is to be unpredictable in your routine; that way, the horse must look to you for direction instead of trying to assume he knows where to go. A reining trainer will rarely practice patterns.

He will practice the individual maneuvers, but rarely puts them together into regular patterns. The American Quarter Horse Association has only about a half-dozen reining patterns, and even the dumb horses start to figure them out after a while! The diagrams on page 70 illustrates horse movement that is not on the line and how this movement might be corrected. Through your knowledge of natural aids, you can probably think of other ways to correct these situations. Remember that every horse is different and might require a different approach. Mental equitation emphasizes creative problem solving.

Executing a Straight Line

With both hands centered, hold the horse's head directly in front of his body. Your weight should be centered, except when you shift weight to the opposite direction to correct for drift. Your legs should be at the girth, holding each side and creating a corridor on the line of passage. They can be used in the forward or back positions to put the horse back on the line if he comes through your holding leg. Ride the horse between your reins and legs, pushing him straight down the line. You should never need to turn your head or shoulders while you're moving in a straight line.

Executing the Circle or Turn

Always turn your upper body slightly, or *open your shoulders,* toward the inside of the circle. This is important for any turn, but can be practiced easily through your circles. As you sit up tall on your horse, visualize that your body is built around a vertical pole, like a carousel horse. The pole keeps you from collapsing forward but allows you to rotate left or right. If you keep your head up and look where you're going,

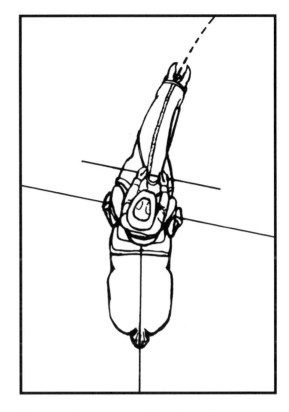

Opening the Shoulders: Through the turn, the rider should rotate or "open" his shoulders to the direction of the turn. The hands automatically follow into a bending position.

the shoulders will follow, and the hands will follow the shoulders. This warns the horse of the upcoming turn, so he stays softer and quieter through the corner.

If you want to prove this to yourself, set up a jump facing a wall of the arena. As your horse jumps and sees the wall in front of him, he'll be looking for a place to go. If you don't open your shoulders as you jump the fence, he will just pick a direction randomly. If it's not the same direction you picked, you may be sucking sand.

Here is a very important piece of advice: *don't turn your head any more than the arc of the turn!* This is one of the most common technical

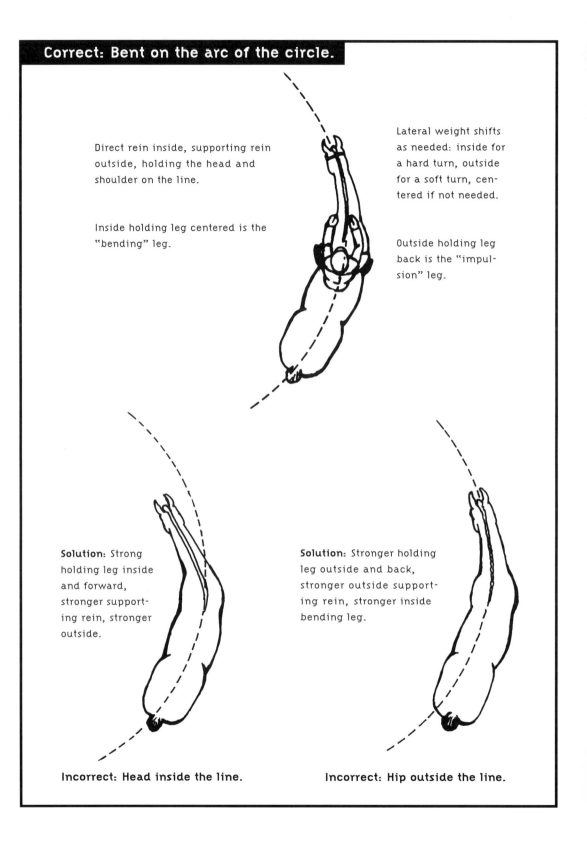

Correct: Bent on the arc of the circle.

Direct rein inside, supporting rein outside, holding the head and shoulder on the line.

Inside holding leg centered is the "bending" leg.

Lateral weight shifts as needed: inside for a hard turn, outside for a soft turn, centered if not needed.

Outside holding leg back is the "impulsion" leg.

Solution: Strong holding leg inside and forward, stronger supporting rein, stronger outside.

Solution: Stronger holding leg outside and back, stronger outside supporting rein, stronger inside bending leg.

Incorrect: Head inside the line.

Incorrect: Hip outside the line.

problems I see in advanced lessons and horse shows. Some riders look toward the center of the ring during the entire class! Most instructors teach beginners to open their shoulders by having them look into their turns. However, when riders get more advanced, few are told that the important technical movement is actually in the shoulders, not the head.

Although you should be able to look around the ring without moving your shoulders, it is easier to open the shoulders when the head is turned in the same direction. I tell my riders to turn their heads at the same angle as the horse's head and neck. Doing so keeps the head straight most of the time, turning only on the arc of the circle through the turns. Likewise, this helps to open the shoulders more noticeably as the turn becomes tighter.

The following aids are typically used to ride through a circle or turn:

- The rider opens his shoulders in the direction of the turn.
- Direct inside rein (or neck rein) turns the horse's head on the arc of the circle.
- Outside supporting rein prevents the head and neck from overbending on the arc.
- The inside leg holds at the girth, preventing the horse from spiraling into the center of the turn.
- The outside leg holds behind the girth to keep the hip from fishtailing outside the turn with his hip. (Both holding legs are *inactive*.)
- The rider's weight aids should be helping the horse stay balanced as he leans into the circle, preventing him from spiraling inside or outside. Normally, the rider will shift his weight inside on a tight turn or keep it centered on a wider turn.

Executing a proper circle, with the horse bent in the arc of the turn. The rider's shoulders are slightly opened to the turn, inside holding leg centered, outside holding leg back, inside direct rein, and slightly lateral weight displacement.

A BAD EXAMPLE! Overbending inside the arc of the circle and leaning too far inside with the upper body.

The "shoulder-in" is one of the "two-track" lateral suppling exercises. With a left direct rein, left displacing leg at the girth, and right passive seat, Erika is moving in the direction of the arrow. Notice the horse crossing over in the front to stay on the forward track.

IMPULSION

Impulsion is one of those hard-to-explain concepts that students sometimes confuse with forward speed. Impulsion is the speed of the horse's response, a sort of energy reserve. It is a quick, quiet, and cooperative reaction to the rider's aids. A horse moving with impulse should look willing, alert, and energetic. He should have the attitude of a showhorse.

Suppose you were ten years old again, watching *The Brady Bunch* on television, and your father casually said to you, "Could you please come here for a moment?" (If you were like my son, response time could be measured in commercial breaks.) Now suppose he called you like this: "Hey, you lazy hide, get your sorry butt over here right now!" You would probably react differently! You would be moving with impulsion.

Don't get the wrong idea; I don't want you to override your horse. That just makes him nervous and cranky. You can be assertive with your aids *and* sensitive to the needs and feelings of the horse. Remember—you don't *make* a 1,000-pound horse do anything, you *convince* him to do it. You sell him on the idea that he should cooperate with you. Some riders are better salesmen than others, but everyone can improve their sales skills.

As with any type of sales, you need to get the "customer" excited about the product, and this just comes naturally to some people. A positive attitude conveys confidence in yourself, and a businesslike approach keeps both horse and rider focused on the task at hand. The horse can feel when you are enthusiastic, and it pumps him up, too. To get your horse moving with impulse, don't be timid with your aids.

In the moments before a reining class, this horse captures the spirit of "impulse"—reserve of energy, and the willingness to use it.

DEVELOPING LONGITUDINAL AGILITY

Hopefully by now you have noticed that the theories in this book are interwoven in a network of sorts. A deficiency in your knowledge or skill in one area will affect other areas, and I try to impress upon my students that by fixing one problem, you are usually solving or preventing others. Based on the mental equitation system of moving progressively from one skill to the next, a horse that is stabilized, on the line, and moves with impulsion is ready to be finished in longitudinal and lateral training.

LONGITUDINAL AGILITY

Longitudinal agility focuses on the movement of the horse's center of balance along his length. It involves primarily the horse's head and neck, the spine, and the hindquarters. Elevation of the head and neck, increased flexion at the poll, or increased engagement of the rear quarters tend to shift the center of balance rearward. This makes the horse lighter on the front end, more agile and athletic in both longitudinal and lateral movement. Dressage, western reining, and cutting horses are good examples.

Longitudinal agility is the ability of the horse to adjust his length, from head to tail, while in motion. It involves his ability to lengthen or shorten his frame, regulate forward speed and length of stride, and adjust his center of balance along the length of the frame. More specifically, it is the ability of the horse to make the following adjustments (I've listed these in approximate order of increasing difficulty):

This young reining horse demonstrates a mechanical concept used by all well-schooled horses for every downward transition. Stopping with "rear disc brakes" is comfortable. Stopping on front brakes feels like driving your mother's station wagon (the one with the bad shocks).

- *Increase or decrease forward speed without breaking into another gait.* For example, he must be able to go from a slow trot to a fast trot without breaking into a canter.
- *Raise or lower his head and neck in response to the rider's aids.* For example, he should flex at the poll and raise his head in response to collection of the snaffle reins and urging from the rider's legs and seat. Raising or lowering the head directly affects longitudinal agility by moving the horse's center of balance backward or forward.
- *Adjust the stride to emphasize vertical engagement rather than horizontal engagement.* For example, this would be the ability to perform in an event like Hunter Under Saddle (where the stride should be long, sweeping, and ground covering), and then perform in Western Pleasure (where the horse moves with a short, balanced, and agile stride).
- *Adjust center of balance forward or rearward while in motion.* This involves raising or lowering the

horse's head, increasing or decreasing horizontal engagement.
- *Lengthen or shorten stride, without affecting forward speed.* For example, when the judge asks for an extended trot, he expects to see an increase in horizontal engagement and thus a lengthening of stride. It is important to maintain a consistent forward rhythm. Contrary to popular belief, extension does not call for a faster rhythm.

HORIZONTAL ENGAGEMENT

Horizontal engagement occurs when the horse reaches forward with his back legs further than he reaches back. Take a look at the vertical line drawn through the horse's hip in the illustration. Because the horse is extending his foot at least as far as he is disengaging it behind the line, we can say he is engaged. Such a stride brings more of the horse's substantial body mass back onto his

With the vertical line drawn in, you can see that the engagement of the hind limb in front of the vertical is at least as great as the disengagement of the opposing hind limb behind the vertical. Therefore, we can say this horse is horizontally engaged.

This horse is not engaged in the rear and is carrying his head "in front of the bit." Therefore, we can say that he is not collected, although he is moving with enough balance that I would guess this to be a momentary lapse as the camera snapped.

In this photo, Matt and his horse demonstrate a nice forward hunter pace at the trot. Notice how much engagement he is showing — both horizontally and vertically. The head and neck elevation pushes his center of balance backward along his spine, like a jumper.

This photo reveals the horse's longitudinal agility at the trot. I've dropped his head, centered his balance, and established less emphasis on vertical engagement. As a result, he is moving more like a quarter horse hunter.

A nice example of a Western horse "on the bit" and "collected." This head carriage gives the horse a very central balance, appropriate for certain Western disciplines.

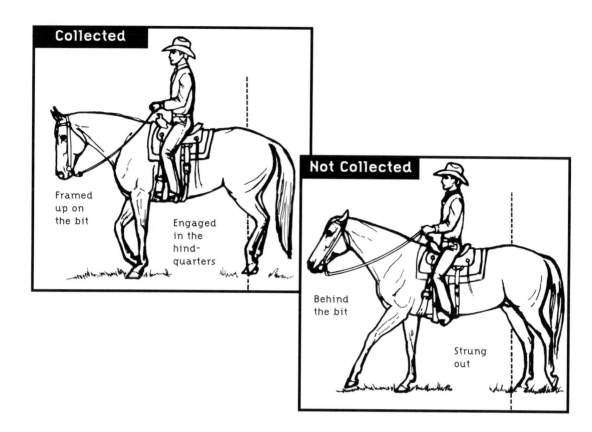

Collected

Framed up on the bit

Engaged in the hindquarters

Not Collected

Behind the bit

Strung out

hindquarters, which lightens the load on the front end. Engagement of the hindquarters is required for any movement that demonstrates longitudinal agility (such as collection, downward transitions, and the halt).

VERTICAL ENGAGEMENT

Good vertical engagement shifts the horse's center of balance toward the rear, flexes him at the poll, and produces slow but highly impulsive forward movement. The more a horse flexes his knees and hocks when he moves, the more he is vertically engaged. Some people say that a vertically engaged horse has a lot of "action" in his stride. Vertical engagement refers to the *quality* of the stride rather than the length, and is

expected of show horses that should exhibit animation in their gaits.

COLLECTION

When it comes to riding horses, lots of people can "point and kick," but advanced riders know how to use aids to "collect" the horse, making him light, agile, graceful, and responsive to the rider's cues. The key to advanced riding is the ability to use several aids simultaneously with the right level of intensity. Any imbalance in aids will result in a breakdown in communication with the horse.

Collection, which involves both ends of the horse, amounts to gathering an eight-foot-long horse into a seven-foot frame. A horse that is collected in the back end is said to be "engaged," rounded in his back, very balanced and agile. A horse that is collected in the front end is said to be "on the bit," carrying the bit quietly and willingly, responsive to the directions given him through the reins. The horse will hold his neck back toward his center by flexing at the poll and neck. A horse is not collected unless he is both engaged *and* on the bit.

To ask for collection, you drive the horse forward with your seat and legs. Your seat asks the horse to drop his hip, allowing his rear legs to swing further forward. Your urging legs ask the horse to lengthen stride, made easier because of the dropped hip. The horse moves forward to take the bit, which you have set as the forward boundary of the horse's movement—the front of his "frame."

In order to maintain collection, you must always use at least as much leg activity as rein activity. A rider who uses too much rein without supporting leg aids will have a horse that is "strung out" (the opposite of engaged).

EVASIONS OF THE BIT

A horse that is evading the bit is not collected. The diagrams show the three most common evasions of the bit.

An example of the first evasion is the lazy horse that refuses to move to the front of the

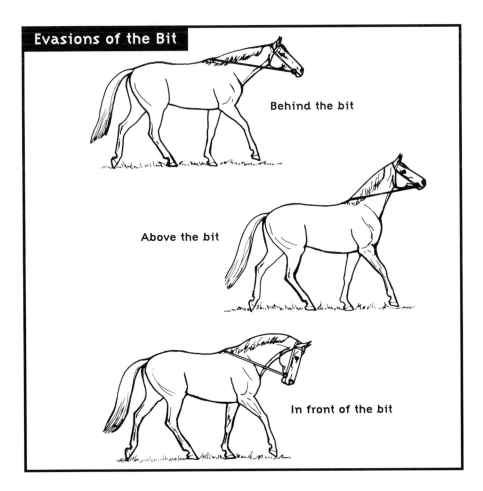

Evasions of the Bit

Behind the bit

Above the bit

In front of the bit

This young horse is evading "in front of the bit," pulling it back toward his chest. Notice the momentary slack in the reins, resulting in loss of contact. The rider feels as though the horse has disappeared.

frame, or goes "behind the bit." He straightens the angle of his poll, and sticks his nose out to the bit, avoiding contact by staying at the back of the frame. Such a horse can have plenty of impulse, but maybe he has never been taught to move onto the bit. Or, he can be lazy and truly evading the bit. The lazy horse must first be taught to move forward, perhaps with long-trotting or cantering in a field on a loose rein. After he gets used to the idea of moving forward with impulse, then the rider can begin to use the hands to set the front of the frame, while continuing to drive the horse forward from the legs. Always remember that whenever you use the reins, you must also use your legs to engage the horse from the rear simultaneously.

The second way a horse evades the bit is to overflex at the poll, pulling the bit back to his chest and getting "in front of the bit." This is usually a sign of a horse that has been schooled with too aggressive rein aids or too severe a bit too early in training. Often, this horse has been schooled extensively with artificial "head-setting" devices and has learned to yield to the bit in the interest of comfort, but has not really learned to carry the bit willingly. He can usually be corrected by riding on a loose rein with a very mild bit in a casual setting. Eventually he will learn to relax once he sees you're not going to crank him in.

The horse that takes the bit in his teeth and

Matt has asked for the left lead in the canter by pushing the horse's shoulder outside with the hands and kicking with the outside leg. By using an inside leg to balance the horse, the outside leg is puching the shoulder out, he holds the outside direct rein and the inside rein to hold the horse's shoulder out without turning his head. Thus asking the horse to take the left lead. We call this "inside-out."

Sometimes this behavior indicates that the horse has problems with his teeth or has a bruised mouth or tongue. Occasionally a horse is best controlled with a stout bit but doesn't have the mouth to handle it. I once had a big Thoroughbred jumper that would grab and run with a snaffle. We figured a pelham would give him some brakes, but then he was afraid to move forward! He was actually afraid of the bit. I compromised by taking the curb chain off the bit completely, which pretty much eliminated the action of the curb rein. He was happy, I was happy, and his rider felt safe again.

TRANSITIONS

Like the automatic transmission of a car, good transitions between gaits provide smooth, seamless changes from one "gear" to the next. Weak or ineffective transitions are like a car with a bad clutch, jerking or straining from one gait to the next. Strong, effective transitions are imperative to maintain forward movement, balance, and collection. Likewise, collection is imperative for quality transitions.

pulls on the reins is also evading the bit. He typically sticks his nose in the air, getting "above the bit," which results in the rider losing all control of the horse's head. Some horses get above the bit just to be stubborn, a situation best handled with artificial aids such as running or standing martingales and draw reins. If a young horse just learning to carry a new bit uses this evasion, evaluate the bit first. Maybe it is too severe for that horse at that particular point in his training. Or perhaps you're asking too much of him, being too aggressive with your hands, given his understanding of the natural aids.

Upward Transitions

All upward transitions begin by getting the horse's attention. Let's say I'm walking on the rail when it comes time to trot. My horse has probably lulled himself into a minor coma, so before I can get a transition, I'm going to have to bring him back from his world of darkness. I could accomplish this by yelling, "Hey, wake up!" but as an advanced rider, I choose something more subtle.

In advanced equitation, one of the most important aspects of upward transitions is called "setting the horse up." In setting up for the walk-to-

Matt demonstrates the second part of the canter transition, which we call "outside-in." His inside leg drops off to give the horse room to move from the outside displacing leg. At the same time, Matt drops his rein hand down and center, while stepping down into his inside stirrup.

trot transition, the rider should have enough rein contact to keep the horse from leaning too heavily onto his front end. The rider should have enough lower leg contact to push the horse's hindquarters up underneath him, making the horse lighter and more balanced in his front end. A light front end helps the horse balance through the transition, preventing him from just lurching forward into the next gear.

I teach a two-step method called "inside-out and outside-in" for setting the horse up for the canter. In the "inside-out" position, all inside aids move to the outside. I'll balance the horse momentarily over his *outside* shoulder by lifting with my

inside leg (as needed) and sitting over my outside leg. At the same time, I lift my reins slightly up and outside, holding them back over the pommel. This lightens the horse's front end and opens the shoulder for the lead.

A split-second later, I drop the horse into the "outside-in" position, with all aids coming from the other direction. I drop my reins into the center position and shift my weight over the inside seat bone. The inside leg has to come off the horse to give him room to move into the lead. (Many riders have a lot of problems getting leads because they hold the horse too tightly with the inside leg.) The outside leg reaches back a little

This photo shows the "inside-out" aids for the left lead canter: left balancing leg, right seat, and rein aids opening the horse's left shoulder. In a fraction of a second, these are followed by . . .

. . . aids for the "outside-in" position. While the outside displacing leg in the back position asks for the transition, the centered reins and inside seat help to balance the horse.

and pushes the horse's hip forward and toward the center of the ring. These inside-out, outside-in balancing positions, used in immediate succession, move the horse through the canter transition with balance, energy, and responsiveness.

After setting your horse up for the transition, immediately follow with the cue. Using various leg and rein aids, try to ask for the transition so specifically that you incorporate the desired speed, length of stride, and level of collection right into your cue. It doesn't really matter what the cue is, as long as you and your horse understand it. Even after the cue, the transition is not complete—

you should immediately set the pace. If you let the horse choose the speed, he will usually choose either "crawl" or "ballistic"!

Downward Transitions

Downward transitions are probably easier to learn than upward transitions because the same ones are used regardless of the gait; they are just applied with different intensity. However, downward transitions are tougher to execute. Besides the mechanical cue, they require some intricate timing and balance.

The half-halt

Although many people think the rein aids are the primary aid in the downward transitions, they are actually a secondary or supporting aid. If you watch some good stoppers (like reining horses), you'll see that the riders hardly even use the reins to stop; instead, they use a technique called the "half-halt."

The half-halt is the first and most basic aid used in all longitudinal transitions. It's important to keep in mind that the half-halt is not a solitary function but a preliminary aid that must be followed closely by secondary aids. It is a kind of pelvic crunch that tells the horse the rider is about to deliver an important message. It's like the motion you used as a kid at the playground to get your swing moving back and forth. I don't know if that move has a name, but you know what I mean—you sort of tip your crotch and push down and forward with your seat. This pushing motion is combined with sitting up tall and straight. It's helpful to think of using your back to help you stop. Use the strong muscles of your back to keep your balance up and help bring your arms back through the transition.

The half-halt asks the horse to hesitate and look for a second aid, sometimes in an attempt to regain control or collection. It is typically used whenever the horse is getting high strung or losing concentration. For example, suppose you are riding a jumping horse that is getting too strong and charging down the line toward the fence. You want to sit up and hold the front end with good bending elbows, settling to your seat to push the horse's tail to the base of the fence. By half-halting, you are making the horse hesitate and drop his hip, and in that instant of hesitation you can use your hands and seat to regain collection and make the adjustment to the fence.

Originally an English technique, the half-halt has been adapted for use by most Western riders, although they might not call it by name. (This is an example of the convergence of styles that I refer to as interdisciplinary horsemanship. Although their terminology may differ, various disciplines employ the same concepts.) Western riders use the half-halt a little differently than English riders because a western horse is typically more engaged in the hindquarters than a hunter, and moves more slowly and conservatively. A Western rider gets that movement partially with a continuing half-halt of sorts. He rides with his seat tucked up under himself, his legs out in front, and his upper body almost behind the vertical. His constant half-halt asks the horse to engage the rear end and slow to the hands of the rider.

The follow-through

When making a transition to a slower gait instead of to a halt, simply use a quicker release of aids while squeezing the legs in your follow-through. Try to move your back, shoulders, elbows, wrists, and fingers as one unit. Using all your joints a little keeps you from having to use any one of them a lot—and makes the transition look much quieter and more effortless.

Just as you do with upward transitions, you should continue giving the cues until you get the desired response. The horse knows what you expect, and it is important that you require the correct response before releasing the aids. Remember that the rein aids we use to slow or stop the horse are uncomfortable for him, and his reward is for you to release the pressure. Transitions to a slower gait are the toughest to execute because of the combination of timing, coordination, and intensity required. The canter-to-trot transition is particularly difficult to do well, and my students practice it a lot to sharpen the skills needed for all downward transitions.

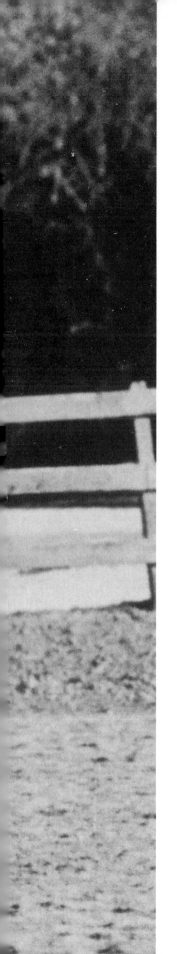

DEVELOPING LATERAL AGILITY

While longitudinal and lateral agility can be developed somewhat independently of one another, most lateral agility requires basic longitudinal skills. Lateral agility is the horse's ability to be flexible and agile from side to side, important for specific movements that include turns on the forehand or haunches, sidepasses, changes of lead, pivots, spins, and so on. The development of lateral agility depends mostly on the horse's willingness to respond to the natural aids.

Specifically, lateral agility involves the following skills (listed in approximate order of increasing difficulty):

- *The ability to respond to lateral aids*. For example, the horse must willingly move away from a displacing leg or neck rein, or toward a lateral weight displacement.
- *The flexibility of the head and neck in response to rein aids, independent of the rest of the body*. For example, while the horse is standing still, you should be able to bend the horse's head and neck around toward your knee. Or, while walking to the left, you should be able to bend the horse's head to the right.
- *The ability to carry himself through circles and turns with his head and body on the line*.

We use all three of these lateral skills to some degree every time we make a turn. Suppose you've just jumped over fence number four on the diagonal line, and you need to roll back to jump fence number five on the opposite diagonal. You would push your horse out into the end of the ring

This horse is balancing up for a spin to the right. You can see his right hind foot reaching forward to take the weight, and his left front foot beginning to cross over the right. Notice how he bends right from the two-handed neck rein.

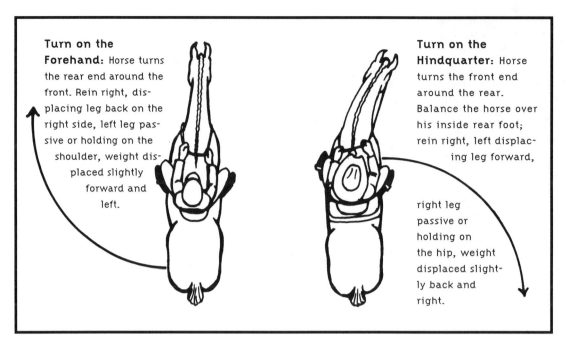

Turn on the Forehand: Horse turns the rear end around the front. Rein right, displacing leg back on the right side, left leg passive or holding on the shoulder, weight displaced slightly forward and left.

Turn on the Hindquarter: Horse turns the front end around the rear. Balance the horse over his inside rear foot; rein right, left displacing leg forward, right leg passive or holding on the hip, weight displaced slightly back and right.

Lateral Movements

with your inside leg for several strides, holding your horse out of the turn until you had a good angle of approach to the next fence. When you reached the line of approach to fence number five, your emphasis would change from a holding inside leg to a displacing outside leg, preventing a bulge to the outside of the jump. Throughout this turn, you would keep the horse bent on the arc with rein aids and balanced through the turn with lateral weight aids. All these aids are asking for a particular lateral response. When you put all the individual responses together, they form a smooth and balanced turn to the jump.

THE TURN ON THE FOREHAND

The most basic lateral movement, and therefore the one I teach first, is the "turn on the forehand." In this movement, the horse must plant his front feet while turning the rear end around them. This

simple lateral movement is the only one that requires the center of balance to be over the forehand, the horse's natural carriage of balance. To observe such a turn, watch a horse walking along the fenceline in a field. When he turns around with his head toward the fence, he will naturally turn on the forehand.

The turn on the forehand is most easily done at a medium walk. Some consider it a forward movement since the horse needs to keep his weight moving forward over the forehand. When done on the rail, the horse should turn his head to the outside (toward the rail) and the hip to the inside (away from the rail.) This movement can be executed to different degrees (for example, one-fourth, one-half, or three-fourths of a turn on the forehand.)

With a horse tracking left on the rail, the rider should sit up on the vertical, with weight shifted slightly to the left. He should have a right displacing leg slightly back on the horse's barrel, and a left holding leg at the shoulder. A direct or neck rein will turn the head to the right, opposite the hip, with an outside supporting rein holding the head and neck straight ahead. He should use his leg rhythmically (instead of constantly) to keep the horse relaxed but attentive to the aid.

Horses frequently walk forward out of a turn, indicating that the rider needs to sit up and hold with the reins. A horse that backs away from the turn needs more urging legs on both sides. And a horse that rubbernecks into the turn needs more supporting outside rein and lots more inside leg.

THE TURN ON THE HAUNCHES

The "turn on the haunches" is a movement in which the horse sets his inside rear foot, turning his front end and the other three legs around the inside rear. For Western horses, the turn on the haunches is used for everything from a reverse on the rail to the lateral movements of reining or cutting classes. It is more difficult than a turn on the forehand because the horse naturally stands with sixty percent of his weight on the forehand. Therefore, before he can turn on the haunches he has to first shift at least ten percent of his weight to his hindquarters.

When tracking left at a walk, the rider would stop the horse, rock him back onto his left hip, while sitting back on the vertical and slightly to the left seat bone. The inside or left leg would come off the horse to allow him to turn to the inside, while the outside or right leg would push the barrel of the horse to the left. Again, the rider would use his leg rhythmically instead of constantly. He would balance the horse back over his inside rear leg with the reins while the legs move the horse. English riders would use

Here, the horse executes a "pivot" or "turn on the haunches." I am balanced over my left seat bone, trying to balance the horse over his left hip. I am using an active right displacing leg, my left leg giving him room to turn his left shoulder.

both a direct and neck rein to the left, while Western riders would use a neck rein back and left, pulling the reins toward the left shoulder.

Remember to open your shoulders slightly into any lateral move. This additional cue to the horse also helps to open your hands, legs, and seat into the proper inside bending position. You should never look into the turn more than your horse does.

THE PIVOT

Characteristic of Western performance horses, the "pivot" is much the same as the turn on the haunches, except it is performed very quickly. When done at speed, the horse's head and neck bend slightly toward the inside of the turn, providing momentum for the pivot. A pivot may be one-quarter, one-half, or three-quarters of a turn. Another variation is the "spin"— technically the same as the pivot, but allowing for turns of more than three-quarters of a revolution. Typically, reining horses in competition will perform two to four spins in a single movement.

THE SIDEPASS

Done correctly, the sidepass is a lateral movement only, in which the horse crosses right feet over left or left feet over right, keeping his head and neck straight ahead. The rider uses direct or neck reining in the direction of the pass, lateral weight displacement to the same side, and displacing leg centered on the opposite side. As with a turn on the haunches, it's helpful to use your leg rhythmically to keep the horse's attention without allowing him to get stiff against your leg. Sit up and hold with the hands, balancing the horse to the center of his body. If you hold your reins too far forward, the horse will walk forward out of the movement. If you pull them too far back, the horse will back out of the movement.

LEG YIELDING

Leg yielding also teaches the horse and rider lateral balance. As in sidepassing, the horse moves to one side without looking or bending in that direction. But unlike sidepassing, the horse moves forward also; he executes a kind of diagonal forward movement.

The aids for performing a leg yield are much the same as the aids for the sidepass, except that both urging legs work to keep the horse moving forward, while the hands relax enough to let the horse execute the movement. Again, you should use your leg rhythmically, relaxing your hips and knees to keep the horse from bracing against the aid. As with sidepassing, the horse should be carrying his head straight in front of himself, or turned in slightly so that you can barely see the corner of his eye.

THE SHOULDER-IN

The "shoulder-in" demonstrates the horse's willingness to bend around the rider's leg with his head and neck, bringing his front end off the line on command while keeping his rear end on the line. The result is that the horse tracks in three lines instead of two—the outside front foot and inside rear align on a track, while the inside front creates a new inner track. The shoulder-in helps to keep the horse relaxed, flexible, and using his hindquarters with impulsion. It improves his balance and has some practical application if you adapt these skills to movement through a corner.

A direct inside rein leads the front end around your firmly held, bending inside leg, while your outside leg keeps the horse's hip from turning out. Both legs move the horse forward toward your outside hand. One common mistake is to pull the horse's front end too far to the inside, causing the horse to become heavy on the forehand, lose impulsion from the rear, and throw his hip to the outside. A horse that is underdeveloped in his longitudinal and lateral skills might rubberneck, a common problem caused by lack of forward impulsion and lack of response to lateral aids.

This rider has dropped the inside shoulder and is leaning too far into the center of the circle. If you look closely enough, you can see that she is struggling to balance up a horse that is "counter-cantering" — leading with the outside lead.

CHANGES OF LEAD

Although we don't normally think of a change of lead as a lateral movement, it qualifies because of the way the horse shifts his weight. Balance is what leads are all about, as you well know if you ride around a turn on the wrong one!

Simple changes

To ask for a canter, we use a displacing leg because the horse shifts his weight laterally to make the change of lead. We typically use a displacing leg back on the outside to urge the horse to the inside lead. We use the leg in the "back" position because we are actually cueing the *rear* end, which should be first to pick up the lead. When changing leads, the horse will ideally change the

lead on his hind legs first, then follow with his front legs. A "simple change" of leads involves a transition from a canter to a walk or trot, then back to a canter on the opposite lead. The transition to the second canter is executed in exactly the same way as the transition to the first canter.

Flying changes

A "flying change" of leads involves changing leads while maintaining a canter. The horse must change leads during the period of suspension (after the third beat), demonstrating the lateral nature of the change of leads. Moving the horse across the center of the arena to the lead change, the rider balances the horse with the "inside-out" leg and seat aids so he is not leaning into the turn. Then the rider shifts to the "outside-in" position

on the second beat of the canter, moving the horse forward off the outside leg.

Because the horse is most balanced moving forward, you shouldn't back off through the change. Instead, you should sit up, balance the horse deliberately as you approach the lead change, then move forward off the outside leg and the inside seat. Getting your inside leg out of the way of the horse is just as important as displacing with the outside leg. Many riders make the mistake of holding too closely with the new inside leg. This confuses many horses, since you can't use an inside holding leg while you use an outside displacing leg.

Lead changes are much easier if you use the arena to your advantage. The horse changes leads naturally when he changes direction, and he changes direction naturally when the fence line forces him to do so. In the drill I most often use to teach flying changes, the horse canters a half circle to the left on one end of the ring, clears the jump on the southeast corner of the ring, then holds that left bend to canter a diagonal line toward the northwest corner. In this way, even

someone who isn't very good with leads will almost certainly land off the jump on the left lead. (You can do the same drill without the jump.)

I like to think of a flying change as if it were another jump. It is one single, momentary stride at a particular place in the arena. Thinking of it as a jump makes it easier to change the direction, the bend, and the lead all at the same time. I often use a ground pole to teach flying changes, placing it perpendicular to the arena fence line on the northwest corner so the horse will jump it just as he turns right to go down the fence line. If the rider can time that forty-five degree turn to occur exactly at the ground pole, and use the correct aids for the flying change in the air above the pole, the change becomes very natural for almost any horse.

Lateral agility and lead changes are not magical, although to most riders they seem mysterious or elusive. You simply need to understand what you're trying to accomplish and use your imagination to find a method that will make it easy for the horse to be successful. Mental equitation is about learning, thinking, and creating solutions.

Opposite: Compare the previous photo to this one. Here, horse and rider execute a properly balanced bend on the *inside* lead.

 CHAPTER NINE

MENTAL EQUITATION FOR THE SHOW RING

It might be a bit of an oversimplification, but the world of equitation can be divided into two basic groups: recreational riders and competitive riders. Both kinds of riding can benefit from sound equitation, but let's be honest. The two are about as similar as baseball and cricket. Competitive riders dedicate a lot more to their sport than time spent in the saddle or at the barn. They are students of the game. They read and learn all they can about riding, just like you're doing!

From the first riding lesson, every rider works on proper body position and use of natural aids, which are difficult enough to perfect. I can teach almost anyone to ride well. It's much harder to teach someone to show well, because the rider's degree of success will be in direct proportion to his or her *desire* to compete and achieve. The winning difference comes from within.

The bottom line is that you don't become a competitive rider just because you can afford to show. Being successful in the show ring requires that you honestly assess your own ability (and that of your horse) and choose an appropriate level of competition. It requires impeccable attention to detail and striving for perfection in every aspect of your performance. It requires being prepared and having a confident, winning attitude before the judge.

ATTENTION TO DETAIL

The single element that most separates exceptional riders from good riders is perfectionism. The competition at horse shows is keen, and the difference

Proper position without stirrups is exactly the same as if you had them. My team rides at least one-third of their practice time without stirrups to develop leg strength and balance. Not everybody is gifted, but *strength is what you make of it!*

between first and third place can be decided by the smallest of details. The winners are doing *everything* correctly; the others are satisfied to get *most* of it right. You simply cannot be a top rider unless you are a perfectionist—at least in your riding.

If you want to win horse shows, make your practice time count. Don't just go through the motions. The better you get, the more exacting your standards must be. I remember arguing with one of my students who was practicing for the Intercollegiate National Championships. I was getting after her about being six inches out of position at the beginning and end of her pattern, and she thought I was being unreasonable. Grudgingly, she did it over; in fact, she did it several times—perfectly. Three days later she was a National Champion.

WORK ETHIC

Horsemanship, like all sports, requires constant self-discipline and motivation. Competitors in any sport will say that it's more difficult to *repeat* as champion than to *become* a champion. Today's top rider will be average next year if he allows himself to stagnate. No matter how well you ride, never assume you have peaked. Practice with intensity. It is better to take a vacation from your riding than to relax and become a lazy rider. Sometimes taking a break for a couple of weeks is the best thing for you.

There is no easy way to become a winner; you simply must put in the time and the miles. The only way to the top is through hard work and dedication. I have yet to see a top competitor who had less than exceptional work habits. The best riders really push themselves at practice. Practice lots of transitions and individual tests. Practice the things you will be expected to do in a show, including things that are difficult

for you. Don't practice only what you're good at just because it's harder to face your problem areas!

Finally, vary the routine of your training. Don't let the horse assume he knows what's coming next. Varying his routine keeps him responsive to you and interested in his work. The *least* varied work you can do on a horse is to go around and around on the rail! Horsemanship is a constant learning process, and a rider and horse must continue learning to stimulate motivation and concentration. It's a great idea to keep finished horses working on trail obstacles, or learning to jump, since these always present new things to learn. I find this goes a long way toward keeping a fresh, enthusiastic mind in both horse and rider.

PHYSICAL PREPARATION

Equitation classes are judged on both form and function. The most successful entries will be attractive and stylish but also functional and workmanlike. Every discipline has a standard that is found in the association rule book, so do your homework before the show. But remember that knowing what to do is only a start; you will need physical strength in order to do it well. Equitation is a physical sport, and the winners in the long run are the strongest and best conditioned.

Many riders and trainers overlook the value of strong, flexible legs, and thus discount the hard work of riding without stirrups or in two-point position. My riders practice at least one-third of every lesson without stirrups (especially at the posting trot), strengthening the leg muscles that will hold the legs still and provide a strong base for position. We spend nearly as much time at the two-point position, which forces the rider to have her legs back under her body while developing the strength needed to grip and improving

Daddy Jim's Most Important Rules of Riding Position

1. Straight vertical line from ear-shoulder-hip-heel.

2. Straight line from elbow-hand-reins-bit.

3. Toe vertically beneath the knee.

4. Heel lower than the toe.

Below: Folding the hands behind your back forces your shoulders back and opens your chest properly. We can longe with hands in many different positions, each addressing a unique flaw in the rider's equitation.

When working without stirrups, you will want to "cross your irons," pulling the buckle down a few inches before crossing the stirrups.

Many people tend to twist their inside shoulder forward, usually consistently in both directions. This one-handed exercise loosens the inside shoulder, encouraging the opening of the shoulders through the turn.

upper body balance. In addition, two-point strengthens the upper back muscles necessary for correct posture, providing the rider keeps her head up and shoulders pulled back. If you are serious about equitation, there is no way around having correct position and strength to hold that position.

MASTERY OF TESTS

Although considerable variation exists between disciplines, all equitation classes consist of primary work and testing. In standard Hunter

Equitation on the flat or Western Horsemanship classes, group work "on the rail" will be followed by individual testing for the top riders. In Quarter Horse shows, the individual test will usually be done first by everyone, then only the top riders will be called back to work on the rail. In Equitation Over Fences, the test will usually be a spontaneous second, shortened course.

Individual work is a vital part of competitive equitation because it demonstrates absolute rider/horse communication and cooperation. It's not hard to ride a horse around the rail in a group—he'll pretty much follow the others. Think about it. Your horse likes to trot or canter

I often work advanced riders without reins on the rail. I prefer this to longeing because it forces you to relax and trust in your horse—harder than it sounds. Many of my advanced riders can walk from canter, and reverse direction—without hands.

when he sees the others do so. The horse likes to think he knows the routine, and this can become a problem. You don't need to steer much on the rail because he'll turn by himself when he gets to the fence at the end of the arena.

Many riders get into the habit of riding only one side of the horse because a horse won't take off toward the rail. Anything the horse does will be directed *away* from the rail, and as a result many less experienced riders are overly protective of the inside. A rider who is constantly leaning or looking to the center of the ring clearly causes other problems for both horse and rider.

The real test takes place in the middle of the arena, where success depends upon the wits of the rider and cooperation of the horse. The rider must be balanced and symmetrical, while the horse must be balanced, on the line, and responsive to the rider. Many people consider individual

tests the most frightening part of showing horses and the most difficult to understand. The great thing about this situation is that the people who can become good at doing tests have a distinct advantage over the great majority who are scared to death of them.

I see many riders who are exceptional on the rail, but who fall to pieces when asked to perform a simple figure off the rail. I work my equitation students on the rail to polish up the use of legs, seat, and hands, and to work on strength. In addition, we always work off the rail, trying to perfect the students' functional equitation. Real communication with the horse is made out in the open, as it is in an individual test.

Nearly all figure work consists of five basic elements: a straight line, a round circle, a change of leads, lateral work, and a back. A rider who can perform each of these individual elements

This rider is executing a straight line, balanced over both stirrups and both seat bones, with shoulders square and head up. She is holding the horse within his space, riding him between holding legs and between the reins.

especially with an inexperienced rider. To see what I mean, start at one end of the arena and move your horse directly toward a point on the other end. Use your hands to direct the front end of the horse, and your legs to keep the rear end on the line following the front.

The Circle

I've asked lots of trainers to name the most helpful thing one can do on a horse, and nearly all of them said "circles." Executing circles requires detail work from both the horse and rider and helps improve balance, bend, collection, stabilization, use of natural aids, and cooperation between horse and rider. Working in circles separates top riders from their less experienced counterparts.

In competition, a circle must be round, not flattened or oval on one side. Moreover, the horse and rider must stop exactly where they began on the circle. Many riders find it helpful to pick a spot in the center of a circle and ride around it, keeping equidistant from that spot. Others find it more helpful to visualize the circle on the arena floor, or to maintain a constant arc by watching the arena fences.

perfectly can combine them to make almost any pattern used in equitation. The key is perfection of the elements. Begin practicing each maneuver separately, striving to perfect that particular element.

The Straight Line

It sounds easy enough to perform a straight line until you try it. Most horses tend to drift laterally,

The Change of Lead

A change of leads is no problem for most show horses. The trick is to make the change smoothly and at precisely the correct time and place in the pattern. Judges usually require a simple change of leads, such as dropping to a trot or a walk for a couple of strides before picking up the opposite lead. This can be easily taught, progressing from several strides at the lower gait to only two. Pushing a horse for a simple change with fewer

The rider is in the "upright" position, as this photo was snapped just after beat two of the canter. Beat two is the most balanced part of the canter because three feet are on the ground.

than two intermediate strides will risk blowing the second lead, and a judge will be no more impressed by a single-step transition than by a two-step transition. As a judge, I would rather see a rider drop to a trot to make his simple change than drop to a walk, since the trot transitions are more difficult to execute. Remember, it is always better to do an easier movement well than to be sloppy in a more impressive movement.

Lateral Work

A turn on the forehand or a turn on the haunches should be precise, fluidly graceful, and performed with solidly commanding rein and leg aids. Other lateral tests might include the sidepass, leg yielding, shoulder-in or shoulder-out, and so on. I like riders to take the horse through these maneuvers one step at a time, concentrating on precision and

control of the movement rather than speed or flashiness. While doing these or any movements, the rider should sit elegantly and properly, with chin up and eyes always ahead.

Backing

Get your horse accustomed to backing as a routine part of riding. When I am schooling a horse, I like to stop and back randomly from any gait. It makes the horse lighter on the front end and also makes backing a normal part of riding, so it's not a big deal when you are asked to do it in a test. With Western horses, we'll sometimes practice more elaborate backing drills, such as backing a figure-eight around two barrels.

The horse should back willingly, in a straight line. The rider should use his legs to move the horse straight and on the bit, while backing with a steady pull on the reins. Pumping the reins or kicking should be avoided, as it suggests resistance or inefficient communication. Sit up on the vertical, without leaning forward or backward. Hands should be deliberate, but not too pushy. Demand a quick response—but if the horse throws his head or gapes his mouth, you'll know you're asking too much too quickly.

APPEARANCE

One of things that makes me craziest is a rider who comes into a horse show unprepared! The most basic preparation is that of appearance, one of the very few factors that the rider can control. The horse has a mind of his own, the judge determines the pattern and rail work, and nobody can choose their competition. But as a contestant, you have complete control over your appearance, leaving no excuse for clothing or tack that is less than perfect.

As shallow as it may seem, your clothes really *can* make a difference between winning and losing. Show clothes don't need to be overly elaborate but should be appropriately styled and properly fitted. I can't tell you how many good Western riders I have seen with hat creases that have gone out of style or have never been in style. Or how many hunt seat riders I have seen not wearing hair nets, or with hair hanging over their numbers. I see riders who don't bother using silver polish, or who don't realize boots are supposed to be clean. As someone who has shown, coached, and judged, I'll be honest: if you're not dressed and groomed properly, you will *not* get a fair look from the judge. The way I see it, you've spent too much money getting to the show to blow your chances because of shoddy appearance.

Choose a professional tack store carefully—

one that deals with a lot of show people. Salespeople there will be able to show you the latest colors and styles and help you find the best fit. Show-quality clothing is expensive, and you want to be certain you are getting something that will help you look and ride like a winner. Know who you're dealing with, because some stores just don't have people who know what is current, even though they're really nice and try to be helpful.

To make sure you're going to look appropriate, find out who wins the events you want to enter and dress the way they do! Riders who look different are at a disadvantage. Styles vary depending on discipline or association; for example, female hunt seat riders may wear very small and simple earrings and should wear just enough makeup to avoid looking pale. In contrast, female Western riders are expected to be a little more eyecatching, so they often wear big, colorful button earrings and lots of makeup. Hunter riders must always wear gloves, preferably black and leather. In Western shows, gloves are optional.

In the American Horse Shows Association (AHSA), or any hunter association I'm familiar with, women are expected to pull their hair up under their helmets. Loose hair is never good in any discipline because it seems unkempt and unprepared. The hunt seat riders I coach wear what we call the "Marcia Brady" style—hair parted in the middle, pulled back over the ears, then twisted and folded over the top of the head. A hair net or two and some spray holds the hair in place before the helmet goes on. Ponytails or pigtails are okay only for little girls, or in certain breed associations. Female Western riders often wear a traditional Quarter Horse hair style—a short pony tail with a big bow or something that matches their outfit, or a "bun" just under the brim of the hat.

Necklaces or bracelets are never acceptable for horse shows, for either sex. Also (I never used to have to talk about this) any visible body piercing jewelry must be removed before entering the ring. Men should remove any earrings or makeup (another topic that never came up until recently). Men with long hair should pull it all straight up and under their hats. If men have facial hair, it needs to be very neatly trimmed. Although simple, traditional rings are acceptable, a judge recently scolded one of my riders for wearing a thumb ring. In general, judges tend to be very conservative, traditional types who don't like you to look like a rock star!

MENTAL PREPARATION

Technically, mental preparation should begin long before the horse show. The more you know, the more prepared you are to make wise decisions in competition. Some people ride great at home, but just can't think straight in the show ring—the cream will rise, and the curds will fall. When the pressure is on, I tell my riders, "Don't be a curd!" Using mental equitation on a daily basis gives riders the knowledge and confidence needed to win horse shows.

Once the show is under way, it is very helpful to watch classes that are similar to the one in which you will compete. Notice how the judge handles the classes, such as what kind of rail work and tests he uses, and how he pulls the class in off the rail. Know exactly what to expect so you can respond promptly and confidently.

Notice ahead of time if the judge has any pattern in watching the class. Which part of the arena draws most of his attention? Where are his blind spots? In competition, a rider must always know where the judge is looking, what he can see and cannot see. You should know where to go to be seen, and where you can go to hide.

Mental preparation involves planning your

moves before you need to move, knowing where you are going before you get there. A university psychology researcher once divided a group of people who had never played basketball into two teams. The first team was told to practice free throws on the court for an eventual shooting contest, while the second team was told to mentally rehearse without going to the gym. After a period of preparation, both groups performed comparably!

Competitors should ride through the show experience mentally, visualizing every obstacle, and plan how to solve problems or correct mistakes. They should visualize success in the show ring, and then visualize every step of the winning process. Mental imagery prepares the mind for specific situations, which then are handled without anxiety. This allows the rider to maintain a more relaxed and confident attitude throughout the competition.

ATTITUDE

Some people are better competitors than riders, competing consistently beyond their ability. They always seem to have their best rides in the show ring, and they carry an attitude into the ring that the judges just can't resist.

If you want to show your horse and win, you must learn to be relaxed and confident—something only preparation will enable you to do. Tension is perceived as fear, apprehension, or uncertainty. A judge looks for a rider who can face and handle situations calmly and confidently, one who is consistently self-assured, whether having a great ride or dealing with a problem horse. To project a confident, winning attitude, a rider must absolutely believe that he can and *should* win every class in which he competes.

A little thing like direct eye contact with the

judge can be effective in projecting that winning image. If nothing else, at least you know that the judge has seen you. How many times have you wondered if you were just overlooked? Try to make eye contact when the judge is watching you back your horse, or while the judge is giving directions for a test or pattern.

For many good riders, overcoming the initial tension is a problem; after the first couple of times around the arena, they can relax. I often tell riders to stop before entering the arena, take two deep breaths, and shake the tension out of their hands and legs. Tension creates a very apprehensive image and affects the horse's performance.

Some riders concentrate too hard rather than relying on skills that have become second nature. For example, many jumpers tend to overanalyze every fence, as they were taught to do as beginners. These riders "think too much" and need to divert their attention. Keep thoughts simple and trust what you know. If you have prepared well, your instincts will carry you farther than you think. Some people find it helpful to keep in mind a favorite song. Some of the riders on my team even think about their studies, or some silly distraction like the latest *Baywatch* episode (remember, these are college students).

Above all, maintain a certain self-confidence in all that you do before the judge. A winning image is a confident image, with head held high and just a trace of a smile. The judge must not see your flaws, your humanness. Instead, he must see a solid, unshaken confidence that says, "I am your winner. Pick *me*!"

SHOWMANSHIP

A horse show is just that—a *show*. The winner is not always the best rider but is the person who put on the best show that day. Don't be afraid to be dramatic, or elegant, or anything else that may help you stand out. Many of the best riders take on a "show stopper" demeanor that is normally out of character for them. Johnny Carson is reportedly incredibly shy, yet he made a great living as host of *The Tonight Show* for several decades, coming out of his shell every night long enough to perform.

Your first responsibility in the arena is to make yourself seen. A good way to do this is to pass before the judge alone on the rail, so you aren't competing with others for attention. By cutting corners or speeding up, a rider can advance his rail position. Going deep into corners, slowing, or circling will move your relative rail position back. Make sure you do this quickly and inconspicuously. Some riders spend too much time circling in the corner for rail position, wasting time that should be spent in front of the judge. If you are stuck in a bunch, be sure you are closest to the judge when you pass.

Hunt seat judges don't mind at all if you start jockeying for position. In fact, many judges seem to *like* it when you get in off the rail and start cutting across the middle, or down the quarter lines. It shows the judge that you're working your position.

In contrast, Western judges tend to want you to stick to the rail more. It's kind of taboo in the Quarter Horse world to circle in the middle, because it makes you look like you're passing people. This gives the appearance that you're not completely controlling your horse, even if you are. For years, the top Western pleasure horses were the smallest horses, because they were naturally short-strided and therefore the slowest movers. All in all, you'll need to be a lot more discreet with your jockeying in a western show.

When jockeying for better position on the rail, move smoothly, quickly, and efficiently to keep your horse out of trouble. It's very discouraging to have a good ride but finish out of the placings because another horse kicked at yours, or you got boxed in behind a slower mover. Most of these incidents are avoidable, if the rider knows his exact relative position and speed in the arena, and works to maintain that good spot on or off the rail.

I like for the students I coach to be either first or last into the arena. This separates them physically from the crowd and automatically registers an impression with the judge. The judge subconsciously takes special interest in the first rider, as an indication of the quality of the class. He is also interested in the last rider, as his cue to begin judging. Try to get in the gate first, although you may find others in a hurry to do the same. The rider who leads the way must be in perfect form when he makes this lasting first impression.

The most critical periods of the class are during the first trot and early in the last canter. Placing the class is mostly a process of elimination; a judge will note certain riders immediately at the walk and first trot, and will eliminate others. He will continue to whittle down this group at the first canter. By the change of direction, the judge has picked the best seven or eight riders, and knows which are in the top placings and which are on the bottom. Finally, the class will be placed in order during the second trot and canter. Sometimes you may have a pretty good ride overall, but if you had problems during these critical periods you still may not place well.

Consistent winners seem to have a flare for showmanship during these critical moments. They know how to make great first and last impressions. Late in the last trot or early in the last canter they become almost theatrical, framing the horse on the bit with impulse, carrying themselves with elegance and presence, and dramatically making "the big pass" before the judge—the

pass that will make or break their chances. Some very good riders are too afraid to take those kinds of risks, content with a third or fourth place. You can't ride conservatively if you want to win the big classes.

Although important, the performance of the horse becomes secondary in equitation. Remember that showing in equitation means that the rider is showing *himself*. Many riders become overly concerned with schooling or training in the show ring, and ultimately detract from their own image. It is important to keep the horse moving with collection and impulsion, but a rider should do only enough show ring schooling to make the horse easier to ride and more ideal for equitation.

I never advise a rider to adjust his overall riding style to accommodate a particular judge. Some judges may like to see a horse move out a little, or see a rider with a shorter rein, and riders may try to adjust for this kind of thing. In the long run, however, a classic, conservative riding style will be appreciated by most judges. When a rider changes styles suddenly, it tends to interrupt his concentration and allows mistakes to occur where they usually would not.

Remember that you are showing your horse to the judge, whose opinion is the only one that counts. With fifteen riders in a fifteen-minute class, you may have about sixty seconds to make an impression. Make the most of those few seconds. Do any schooling or adjustments behind the judge's back. What a judge doesn't see can't hurt you, and what a judge *does* see must be absolutely perfect!

INDIVIDUAL PATTERNS

Many riders find that understanding the instructions are the most difficult part of individual work, and some judges use this fact to identify the best competitors. They give complex instructions that only the sharpest and most experienced riders will be likely to follow correctly.

Unfortunately, many riders make two mistakes before they even begin individual work: they memorize instructions, and they make assumptions. Instead, you should run through the pattern in your mind, exactly as it was stated. If the pattern doesn't work out properly in your mind, stop and ask the judge to repeat or clarify. Know exactly what is expected before riding the test. Judges are happy to answer questions or clarify instructions, but once the first rider begins, it is too late to ask.

Never rely on watching another rider. Don't assume another rider is correct if he performs the pattern differently than you would. You must be your own authority. I don't know how many times I have seen the first rider perform incorrectly, only to have several other people in a row do the same thing. Be confident that you know exactly what is correct and expected.

While the rider before you is working his pattern, move your horse into position to begin. Have yourself and your horse situated and prepared so that you can begin as soon as the judge turns and gives the cue. This is time-consuming work, and a judge is annoyed with a rider who wastes his time. However, don't begin until you get the cue, or the judge may miss part of your performance.

It is important to remember that pattern work is the advanced test of communication between rider and horse. I urge riders to get a little extra control with a shorter rein while they are working the pattern, especially if they will be asking the horse to perform a back or lateral move.

A rider must be sure that his horse knows what is expected. It is useless for the rider to

know the test perfectly if he cannot convey his thoughts to the horse. The riders I coach strive for a slow, steady, deliberate pattern, pausing between any two parts. If you falter, try to get back into position, regain composure, and try again. Corrections are better than failures, but remember you are under somewhat of a time limit.

Individual work should be done very deliberately. Many riders tend to rush the horse through pattern work. Remember that a horse is not the most intelligent of animals and can process only one thought at a time. Before asking a horse to pivot or back, you should stop the forward movement, letting the horse clear his mind of both the forward and stopping motions. Then ask him to perform the pivot or back.

A major part of a winning image comes from the perceived relationship between horse and rider, and treating the horse disrespectfully is the fastest and easiest way to lose the respect of peers. There is nothing to gain by a show ring thrashing. A poorly behaved horse should be quietly, inconspicuously reprimanded, or removed from the ring if it is hindering the performances of others.

PERSPECTIVE

Although many good riders find it difficult to accept an unfavorable decision from a judge, it is absolutely unprofessional to provoke a confrontation with a judge before a crowd of observers. A knowledgeable, advanced rider has little to gain from such a scene and much to lose in terms of image. Good riders consistently do well over a period of time, but nobody wins before every judge, because equitation is subject to personal tastes and preferences.

The best way to become a winner in any field is to emulate the winners, but many riders are too jealous to appreciate someone else's strengths. It may sound funny, but the champions I have known have also been good losers. They understand that there will always be another day, which makes disappointment easier to bear. Likewise, gracious winners are respected for their sportsmanship and compassion. For every winner, there are many losers, so celebration is best done in private.

It's important to remember that when you pay your entry fee, you are actually paying to hear the opinion of the judge, just as everyone else has paid. The decision will be favorable to some and unfavorable to others. Some days you're the windshield, and some days you're the bug! Everybody's entitled to an opinion, but in a show the one that counts belongs to the judge.

Gaited class on the rail. Photo by Dusty Perin.

CHAPTER TEN

MENTAL EQUITATION FOR EFFECTIVE JUMPING

Once, while teaching a group of little girls at horseback riding camp, I asked, "If you could do *anything* you wanted on a horse, what would you want to do?" My eight-year-old daughter suggested, "Read a book?" and all the others said, "Jump." Jumping is what interests most riders. Spend any time around a hunt seat teaching barn, and you'll see that everybody wants to jump. In fact, I'll bet a good number of you skipped the other chapters and went straight to this one! Caught you!

You probably already know that jumping can be a pretty complicated discipline. I could write an entire book just about jumping, so I won't pretend that I can teach it in one chapter. (If you're not already an intermediate or advanced jumper, you might even benefit from reading a good instructional book on jumping before proceeding through this chapter.) This chapter isn't intended to teach jumping from the beginning. Instead, I briefly describe the concepts that make an *advanced* jumper, just as I would do if I were teaching a jumping clinic.

Riders should pursue jumping after becoming accomplished in all the fundamental skills. You wouldn't start jumping before a horse learned to move in balance and stop when asked. Yet, I see college freshmen every year who can't post without stirrups or hold a two-point at a canter, most of whom have already been jumping fences that are three feet high. I even see kids who have been jumping for years and yet can't keep their hands still while posting

Ideally, instructors would hold everybody back until they were ready to advance to specialized skills like jumping or reining. In reality, if trainers

This rider shows very nice angles in her position. She is holding her head up nicely, and she has good rein contact with the horse. However, her foot is too far into the stirrup, and she's pinching a bit with the knee, causing stiffness in her leg. Photo by A. Kumekawa.

109

I start riders and horses over "ground poles" to teach them fundamental techniques on the ground. This is where they learn to adjust length of stride, practice two-point and crest-release, and develop balance.

don't start riders when they want to jump, riders will easily find somebody else who will. Consequently, most instructors start teaching students how to jump before the students have mastered the skills of flat work. I've done it myself. It's a part of the business that's unlikely to change. The challenge is to figure out how to make the most of it.

Here at Miami University, I've had several students who started taking jumping lessons after they were already fairly advanced flat riders. These students learned much faster, retained what I taught more completely, and had a better understanding of the sport than students who weren't as accomplished in the fundamentals when they started jumping. One student began riding as a freshman in a physical education class. She joined Miami's equestrian team as a sophomore walk-trotter and began taking jumping lessons from me during her junior year. As a senior, she took

first or second place in nearly every jumping class all year, won a couple of High-Point Rider awards, and rode over a three-foot course at the Intercollegiate National Championships.

This story illustrates how the intercollegiate system allows riders to compete at their own pace without the expense of owning or maintaining horses. More important, the success of this woman proves that instructors should develop riders slowly, perfecting the fundamentals, and keep them home until they're ready to win! As the saying goes, "Success breeds success."

Jumping is a discipline of action and reaction, of constant mutual communication between horse and rider. If you're talking and your horse isn't listening, you're in trouble, but it works the other way, too. If your horse is trying to communicate something, you need to hear what he's saying. The best riders can learn from their horses as well as teach them. That's why we train at home, on flat work and dressage work besides jumping. You need to understand how your horse reacts when he is out of balance, when you are on his back too much or in his mouth too much, etc. If you know your horse, he'll tell you when you are making mistakes.

Jumping takes a combination of technical skill and bold confidence. For two years at Miami University, I rode with a group called the "Flyin' or Dyin' Monday Morning Aerial Circus." I arranged this group to teach two very talented but timid hunter riders to be aggressive on the jump course. We did some pretty unorthodox stuff, at times displaying little sense and even less fear! The result is that these two exceptional

equitation riders developed into exceptional jumpers. We laughed, learned, and sometimes bled together! In fact, it was during these rides that I formulated many of my interdisciplinary horsemanship and mental equitation theories.

Mental equitation requires that a rider analyze the mechanics of jumping in a logical way, concentrating on those things that help. I find that many trainers overwhelm riders with technical specifics that don't help, just confuse. While other methods might also work, I have found that the techniques in this chapter help most riders perform well because they are basic, nontechnical, common-sense methods applicable to any jump course.

Even though she's a little pinched in her knee and round in her shoulder, this photo brings back great memories of Lisa "K" and the "Flyin' or Dyin' Monday Morning Aerial Circus." Lisa Kostrubanic was Miami University's Team Captain and twice placed second in the nation in the Intercollegiate Horse Show Association Open division. *M. Carlson photo.*

After ground poles, I work inexperienced horses and riders over cross poles like the one pictured here. I prefer cross poles to a low vertical because it teaches horses and riders to jump over the center of the obstacle.

PRACTICE BEING ADJUSTABLE

The key to successful jumping is keeping both you and your horse adjustable. In an instant, you need to be able to sit up, sit back, balance left or right, add or take off leg. Your horse needs to be collected enough to respond by moving up or back, drifting left or right, lengthening or shortening stride, all in response to your aids. For your horse to be that light and responsive, he must be collected, balanced, and moving with impulsion. A good rider maintains collection and impulsion while trying to stay out of the horse's way as he jumps the fence.

I like to work on being adjustable, both on the flat and over fences. The students I coach spend their warmup time adjusting speed, collection, and seat. For the purpose of this interdisciplinary discussion, I use three terms to describe the rider's seat position: two-point,

half-seat, or full-seat. In two-point, which is jumping position, the rider gets her seat off the horse's back so the horse can be more athletic, partly because this position more closely aligns her center of balance over the horse's center of balance. I use the term "half-seat" (not actually a working term) to describe a position that is light in the seat and forward in the hips. The term "full-seat" describes a deeper, more vertical position often used by eventers. (The full seat is not used in the hunter world.)

While you are warming up at the trot, practice a collected, sitting trot, then adjust to a normal working trot. Loosen up at a two-point position. Go to a sitting trot, then canter. Canter at the half-seat, urging your horse up to a good, 12-mph hunter pace. Collect back to a relaxed canter under a full seat. If your horse is being lazy, really get up over your pommel and gallop him forward, all the way around the ring a time or two. That ought to get his blood moving! Practice moving from one speed to another, using a combination of two-point, half-seat, and full-seat.

My students do the same warming up over fences, starting by trotting small crossrails. I want to see a rider canter away from the trot fence. That tells me she is using a solid urging leg off the takeoff spot, through the air, and away from the fence. After that, I usually have riders trot into a line, cantering away to a second fence. Doing the opposite—cantering the first and trotting the second—is even tougher!

It's a good idea to occasionally practice halting between fences of a line. Jump into the line, halt, settle your horse, then canter out of the line. This really teaches a horse to listen to the rider because it is not something that is normally asked. It teaches a rider to ask properly for what she wants, with *all* her aids. If you don't sit down and say "Whoa," the horse will canter down and jump without you.

I also ask my students to practice adjusting to lines. I'll have riders canter the first six-stride line in seven strides, and then I'll have them halt on the end of the ring. Next they'll come forward to do the next six-stride line in six, as it was meant to be ridden. Then we might do it in eight. I ask them to intentionally goof up their striding so they can practice being adjustable. Ultimately, I want my students to learn what each stride feels like. If a rider can recognize her horse's twelve-foot stride, she won't *need* to count strides down the lines.

I also like to have students trot to the one-stride line, then try to *canter out* in one stride. When you go into the in-and-out without momentum this way, you really have to get up over your pommel in a good two-point and power your way out with a strong leg. This drill teaches a rider to be adjustable longitudinally.

I don't mind it when riders sit a horse down in front of a fence occasionally. Many trainers and teachers discourage it, but I like for a rider to make a horse pay attention. It's good to gallop a horse forward to the jump, but ultimately the horse needs to be responsive and under control. He should be able to slow down as well as speed up. If a horse starts getting too wise and charging the fences, I like to see a rider strong enough to sit him on his tail in front of the jump. However, it can become a real problem if a rider stops a horse because of *rider* error. In that situation, you are teaching the horse to refuse to jump when he feels that error.

The kids I coach don't spend much time practicing full courses, partly because I don't want the horses to start thinking they know where they're going. Mostly, I believe that if you can find your spots and adapt your horse to the course, you can do anything on a jump course. I train jumping riders like my friend trains reiners: I have them practice techniques, details, skills. When the time comes to do the full program, they have the specific skills to get the job done.

When they *do* practice a course, I usually let riders take only one shot at it, just like they would do at a horse show. People who want to show need to make their time count when the money is on the line. You can't call "do-over" at the horse show. If my students have problems, I will let them go back and work on specific jumps or parts of the course, not the entire course.

HAVE A PLAN

This may seem fairly obvious to most of you, but in a hunter or hunter equitation class you need to ride the course the way it is written. Somebody hired to design the course spent a lot of time and energy planning, building, and measuring the jump course to make certain it could be ridden exactly as designed. The judge has a written copy of that course, which he might have walked with the riders. He will have an idea how the course should be ridden, and you should too.

First, study the written course. It will show the general configuration of the jumps and the order in which you will be jumping them. The written course may provide information about the distances between fences, expressed either in feet, or—if the course designer was in a good mood when he wrote it—in strides. I would rather see distances expressed in feet so that I can convert them to strides myself. That way, I can factor in the exact length of my horse's stride, which may not be exactly standard length.

Let's say the line is written as seventy-two feet between the first and second fence. A measurement of seventy-two feet means that the average horse at an average hunter pace will canter that line in five strides. Because course designers typically work with a standard twelve-foot stride, it might be easy to conclude that the distance between the first and second fence equals six strides. However, you need to save a half stride (six feet) for landing off the first fence, and another half stride for takeoff to the second fence. Therefore, you must subtract a whole stride. The seventy-two-foot line converts to five strides. You can check your answer by calculating it this way: "Five strides times twelve feet equals sixty feet, plus six feet landing, plus six feet takeoff, equals seventy-two feet."

Next, you need to refine your plan by walking the course. Most shows allow a certain amount of time for everyone to walk the course together. If the written course did not specify distances, this is the time you should measure them for yourself. Practice stepping off a yard at home. (It's not hard, but you do need to practice. I laugh when I see everyone stepping around together in giant steps,

and then arguing about the actual distance because they can't agree on how many steps they counted!)

If you can step off an accurate three-foot step, then you can measure out four steps to a stride. Don't forget to put two extra steps on each end that you won't count in your striding. For example, starting at the base of the first jump, and finishing at the base of the second, I would count this way: "One, two. One, two, three, one. One, two, three, two. One, two, three, three. One, two, three, four. One, two, three, five. One, two. The line is a five-stride," I would declare (and I would be correct!).

If the written course includes the number of strides or feet, I would step off one line anyway, just to make sure I'd checked it out. Riders in intercollegiate shows often have a chance to watch some horses school over the actual course. After seeing the horses making the distances down the lines, I don't worry too much about counting strides.

Perhaps more important when walking the course is to get out into the ends, walking the corners to see how the lines will look upon your approach and departure. Judges like to see equitation riders using the inside leg to push the horse out into the ends of the arena. Stick to the rail for as long as you're able because that gives you and your horse the longest and straightest possible look at the line. Make sure you keep your eyes on the line. As a judge, I hate to see riders running past the approach and having to come back to it.

If you have broken lines or rollbacks, this is the time to walk those turns and see how they'll look. You will want to step off any broken line that looks to be less than four or five strides. Walk it as you think it would be comfortable to ride; I prefer a straight line from one fence to the other if that will work. If the course has an awkward distance when ridden in a straight line (for example, three-and-a-half strides), then you'll need to bend the line a bit to make it ride in four. I don't like to see riders charging a broken line to make it work. Make it ride comfortably for your horse.

Sometimes you'll see people doing silly things like counting strides through the ends. Don't waste your time this way! Remember, keep it simple. Don't try to be a rocket scientist. (If the rocket scientist starts beating you consistently, *then* we'll begin to wonder what she knows that you don't!)

TRUST THE COURSE

Always keep in mind that the jump course is supposed to work! People who know what they're doing have carefully planned and measured the distances to make sure that they will ride well. Let that work to your advantage. All you have to do is determine how close your horse is to the average. If you can find a twelve-foot stride, and remember it well enough to keep your horse on that pace between fences of a line, then you will be a fairly good jumper.

As you probably know too well, it doesn't always work that way. Sometimes your horse will come off the pace between fences, or he won't exactly find the spot at the first fence of a line. That should tell you something as a rider: you need to make an adjustment, and fast, before you reach the next fence! The best riders have computers in their minds that calculate adjustments as needed. If you jump in short to the first fence, or let your horse die off pace as he hits the ground after the jump, you'll need to lengthen his stride between fences. That is, you'll need to *extend* his stride longer than twelve feet for a couple of strides to make up for being short to the first fence. If you jump in really big, or your

horse charges the first one, you'll need to sit up and say, "Whoa, whoa, whoa," in rhythm with your horse's stride, collecting back to get the second fence in stride.

The course is designed to work if you ride at a medium pace, with a medium-length, twelve-foot stride all the way around, and if you find a good spot from which to jump every fence. If things start to go wrong, you can't expect to keep riding as if nothing happened. You'll need to adjust someplace else to keep yourself in the game.

A medium hunter-pace canter for most horses is 10 to 12 mph, which is faster than your canter in hunter under saddle or equitation on the flat. In those classes, you have a little more collection, and might expect to canter at about 8 mph. If you slow to 8 mph on the jump course, you can expect your horse's stride to be shorter, and the five-stride line is going to ride about five-and-a-half. At the other extreme, if you start galloping around at 14 mph, your horse's five-stride line just might turn into a four-stride line, and the one-stride, in-and-out will end up being a bounce. If you keep your pace, your stride will probably stay consistent. The course is designed to work for you, provided you find your takeoff spots.

RIDE WITH IMPULSION

One of my pet peeves is the rider who tries to get too cute. You know the type—loping around the jump course looking like they're going to stop any second, plunking over the fences like a ballerina in slow motion. Just like a baseball pitcher trying too hard to aim the ball, you're going to get yourself in trouble if you try to finesse the jump course.

You need to always be moving forward toward something. In our flat work, my students

This rider is a little top-heavy, her heels coming up a bit and her knees a little too straight. This puts her too high and forward over the horse. Also notice the slack in the rein. Photo by A. Kumekawa.

practice collection by sitting up and moving the horse's rear end forward into their hands. I talk about riding the horse "from your leg to hand," or "in front of your leg." What I mean is that the horse gets his power and impulsion from his rear end, and it's your job to squeeze that energy forward up through your legs into the bridle, so your hands can control collection and forward movement.

If your horse is moving with impulsion, you should always feel as though you're holding him back with your hands. In other words, you are always riding forward from your legs into your hands—with one exception. *When you come to the jump, you need to release with your hands so your horse can have his head and neck to balance himself.* At that moment, you are no longer moving forward into your hands, but you don't take your leg off your horse in midair, either. You keep moving forward from an urging leg, supporting the horse forward

over the fence. You ride the horse's rear end to the base of the fence to make him jump up vertically. A horse that jumps off his forehand jumps "flat" and drags a lot of rails.

When you touch the ground, you should be sitting up, picking up your reins, and again moving forward into your hands as you push away from the fence. As you can see, you are always moving forward on the jump course, first to your hands, then to the fence, then back to your hands.

A horse balances himself at the canter by going forward. Unless your horse is exceptionally talented, you can get yourself into a lot of trouble trying to back him off the fence too much. Attack each fence with impulsion and forward-moving balance. If you canter down the lines to your fences ready to jump, your horse will be balanced, comfortable, and eager to jump.

Often, riders who are uncomfortable with the

Yowza! This rider is doing the opposite—she's not off her horse at all! Her leg is so far forward that she can't stand up in her stirrups, and she is about to catch the horse in the mouth. Photo by A. Kumekawa.

Once again, the rider's foot is too far into the stirrup. You can see how the closed knee results in a bit of a jolt in her landing, as she braces against the impact all the way through her back and arms. Photo by A. Kumekawa.

This horse and rider are demonstrating a nice balanced approach one-half stride in front of the jump. The rider is in a good forward canter over the pommel, "flyin' or dyin'" just the way I want her to do! At the same time, she has a good forward seat, with enough contact to sit up and balance if the horse decides to stop.

hunter pace try to sit back too much. Remember your fundamentals of centers of balance; get yourself up over the pommel and let your horse go forward. I teach riders to canter between jumps in a very light, forward seat—not in a two-point position, but definitely not a full seat either. They can always move up to the two-point when they get to the jump. I don't believe in cantering from a full two-point because some horses will stop occasionally, and I want my students to be able to sit back when needed rather than falling on top of Trigger's head!

BALANCE YOUR HORSE

Dressage riders spend a lot of time working on the horse's balance. Yet, even though fundamental

training often leads riders from dressage into the jump ring, we don't talk as much about balancing a jumping horse. Instructors work hard to get the *rider* balanced over the horse (practicing the two-point, crest-release, and landing), but we sometimes forget about balancing the *horse*. That's a mistake. It doesn't matter if you find your spot and have your striding if your horse is off balance every time he gets to the fence.

Over the years, I've seen a few exceptional riders who can get a horse balanced to every fence, even if they can't tell you how they do it. Some people call it having a "feel" for a horse, but it goes beyond collection and pace, stride length and spots. Other people call it having a good "seat," but lots of people can sit a horse pretty well. The techniques that most people spend years perfecting on the flat just

Here we have a front view from a half-stride out. The pair are vertically balanced, on the line, balanced up, and ready to jump from the right lead canter.

come naturally to some people over fences.

Remember to ride between fences on the jump course. Whenever possible, your horse should go to every jump "on the line," with his head in front of him and centered on the jump. You should ride your horse through the jump course "between your legs" and "between your hands," so that he moves straight ahead as he jumps. It is really challenging his athleticism to ask him to jump on the bend. You want to ride your horse "over his legs," or balanced equally over all four corners of his body. Try to balance him through the turns, without leaning too far into the turn, or "bulging" out of the turn.

Since you know what your course is, you know which lead will get your horse to each fence in balance. If you could jump all your jumps in a straight line, it wouldn't matter which lead you had. Of course you can't, but there are two ways to ask for your leads on the jump course. First, you can ask your horse for the landing lead while he is in the air *over the jump*. Second, you can land on a random lead, then ask for a simple or flying change *at the end of the arena*.

Neither of these techniques works unless your horse is balanced, so it is important to get to the jump balanced, then hit the ground balancing the canter away from the jump. If you take off from a bad spot or come in off the line, you can't ask for a lead over the fence. If your horse is not going with forward impulsion, you can't get the flying change. Lead changes are all about changing balance laterally. So your most important priority is to get your horse to the fence in good balance.

This young rider has "dropped him," or released with the hands too early. The horse didn't stop *this time*, but you can see from the slack in the rein that this doesn't do your steering any good. When you stop steering on a jump course, bad things happen!

Changing Leads Over the Jump

If your horse is balanced to the jump, you can change his balance *in midair* to make him land on the lead you choose. This is the best way to get leads, if you're good enough to do it without pulling him off the line or off balance. As your horse pushes off the ground and hangs in the air over the jump, you must accomplish two changes of balance. The first is to affect your own balance to the inside—the side that will become the new leading leg. Turn your head very slightly to the inside and look in the direction of your new lead. This slight turning motion will help you drop your inside shoulder slightly down and back, thus creating a "passive lateral weight displacement." Don't lean to the side. All the movements in this discussion should be just an inch or two, virtually

unnoticeable to the observer.

By dropping her inside shoulder down and back an inch and closing her inside elbow an inch, the rider will be creating a slight direct rein inside. It's important to have an inside holding leg more or less on the horse's side at this point to encourage him to land on the bend, instead of turning as he lands. With an inside holding leg and inside direct rein, the rider can effectively turn the horse's head and neck a couple of inches to the inside, placing his balance over his inside shoulder. The combination of rider and horse balancing slightly in the same direction is enough to balance the horse over the inside shoulder upon landing, and with any luck the horse should move away on the correct lead.

Unfortunately, many riders aren't subtle enough with midair changes to keep from pulling the horse off balance. The idea is to *change* balance, not *lose* balance. When a rider gets hung out too far over the inside shoulder, it causes the horse to swing his hip out as he lands. If he's off balance, he must compensate in some way. When a rider bends the horse in too much, he's liable to pull the horse off the line entirely.

Some people whose horses do perfect flying lead changes don't worry about changing their lead over the jump. Instead, they wait to do a flying change at the end of the ring. My advice is, try to get your lead in the air whenever possible. If you can get the lead over the fence, you can forget about it and concentrate on the next line of jumps. (As Forrest Gump would say, "That's good . . . one less thing.") If you try and miss on this opportunity, you always have another try at a flying change in the corner. If you wait to change leads in the corner and you miss, you've blown your only chance. Unless your horse is absolutely automatic, it seems to me to be a matter of probabilities. Why not give yourself the most chances at success?

This rider is setting up a right lead in the air. Looking right, she drops her right shoulder and bends the horse around her right leg. Upon descent a split second later, she'll drop her right leg down and forward, freeing his shoulder for the lead. (These cues are a little overemphasized for the camera.)

Performing Flying Changes

Flying changes are a little more complicated than changes over the jump because you are dealing with the momentum of the horse's balance working against your aids. It's easier to affect the horse's balance when he's suspended over a jump. There's not as much he can do to resist, and he hits the ground balanced. In contrast, with his feet on the ground and moving forward at the canter, the horse has his own ideas about balance, and sometimes they don't jibe with your own. Nevertheless, you cannot have a hope of success in the bigger hunter shows without reliable flying changes. Therefore, flying changes have become an important part of jumping.

Some horses dislike flying changes. Maybe they were scared once, or maybe they just aren't confident enough in their own balance. Perhaps they're not confident in the way they are asked for the change, and they think it might be safer to keep their feet securely on the ground. For whatever reasons, some horses and some riders aren't very good at flying lead changes.

Although I don't go into full detail about flying changes in this book, I cover the basics in the chapter on longitudinal and lateral agility. If you're not an advanced rider you may need to do your homework before you'll be able to follow the discussion in this chapter. To do flying lead changes in the jump course, you'll need to remember several things.

First, you can't change leads without changing lateral balance and bend. You have to change lead, balance, and bend all at once, and you must move all three of these elements across the center of the horse. In other words, you can't change bend directly from left to right, although that is how it is described. You really are changing from left to center, then from center to right. Similarly, your horse has to balance vertically momentarily before he can shift balance from left to right. As a rider, you'll feel the horse lift up under your seat as he shifts his balance into the new lead. Your consciousness of the idea of "center" will help you to shift more effectively from side to side.

Second, your horse can't change leads in the middle of a stride cycle. The canter is a three-beat gait with a diagonal pair on beat two, followed by a period of suspension after beat three. *Your horse can't change leads until he gets to the period of suspension.* Ideally, he will leave the ground on one lead, and return to the ground on the other lead. However, sometimes it doesn't work that way. If his timing isn't right, he will "crossfire" or "cross-canter" on a different lead in the front than behind. If he tries to shift his feet too late in suspension, the horse will usually come down on the new lead in front, but with the old lead behind. Most horses, especially with a little coaxing from the rider, will go ahead and change the rear lead on the next cycle.

Crossfiring should tell you that one of two things has gone wrong. Perhaps the horse is not quick enough or balanced enough to do the job. Or maybe your cue came in a little too late. Timing is extremely important in asking the horse for a neatly done flying change. Because the horse must change leads during the period of suspension, it's critical to ask him for the change earlier than that, usually on beat two of the cycle. This gives him one full beat (a fraction of a second) to process

the request before responding during suspension.

Think about how the motion of the canter feels as you ride. You feel like you're floating during suspension, and falling on beat one. You are sitting on beat two, and riding forward on beat three. Beat two is really the only time you can effectively ask the horse for anything during the canter.

Collect the horse to the change, as you straighten the bend and the balance. The active urging leg shifts from the outside leg coming into the center, to both legs across the center, to the new outside leg as you change direction. As the bend changes, the new inside leg drops off the girth enough to let the horse open his shoulder into the new lead. Your upper body changes your open shoulders from one bend across center to the opposite bend. Your shoulders bring your hands along for the ride, and your head and balance follow the general change of direction. One moment later, you change your active leg and bending hand, and shift from one seat bone to the other.

Finally, you have to keep the horse moving forward through the flying change. As you already know, a horse balances himself by moving forward. Slow, collected movement is both artificial and awkward for him. Keep a supporting leg on your horse, and allow him to use his head and neck naturally to balance through the lead change.

Asking for a flying change uses all the natural aids except your voice. Unless you have a clever jingle that you want to recite as you canter across the change, I can't think of any way to use your voice that will be very helpful!

RIDE YOUR PLAN

Once in the ring, ride your plan. If the line calls for six strides, you *can't* ride seven and expect to

Just fooling around on a school horse, Miami University student, Amy Rice, shows the form that made her one of the top collegiate riders in the country. Notice her perfect leg: heel down and knee relaxed open. Her center of balance is stacked above the horse's center, and she executes the more difficult "short release" of the rein.

win in equitation. If you're riding for me, you'd better have a really good excuse (I've already heard most of them) for not going "hell-bent for leather" to get down your lines in the numbers.

Although you can't expect to win if you jump your fences clumsily, you will need to do more than ride fences to win. You will need to get your striding, get your leads, and keep a consistent pace. The best hunter equitation riders *and* the best jumpers are the ones who ride well between the jumps. Worry about your equitation least of all; that should come to you automatically by the time you get to the horse show. Nothing else matters if you don't jump your fences, but I frequently see even experienced jumpers make two common mistakes.

First, many riders try to find that perfect take-off spot that will match their release. That doesn't sound like a bad thing, but it can be. I urge my students to think of jumping in exactly

the opposite terms. Find a reasonable takeoff spot that will work, and adjust the timing and balance of your release to cover the spot. Don't make the spot come to you; you need to go to the spot. A takeoff spot is neither too long nor too short if you see it coming and ride it well. A jumper who makes it look easy is doing a great job of adjusting. That's how it's supposed to look. If it looks hard, you need a little more practice.

The second problem is that many riders have trouble seeing the takeoff spot coming. Since their first jumping lesson, most riders have been taught to keep their eyes up. I taught the same way for a long time, having riders look at the ceiling or beyond the fence as they jumped. The theory is sound; dropping the head is obviously wrong, since it changes a rider's balance. However, you can't jump your best if you don't see what you're jumping.

Amy shows a lot of style at the big show. (She looks like she is trapping flies in her mouth!) To get to this level, you need lots of dedication, perseverance, talent, and money!

While watching grand prix jumpers, I noticed something new. In a class where proper equitation doesn't matter so much, the world's best jumpers very often look down and watch the jump coming under the horse's front feet. Every fence means money to these people, and they don't do anything that won't help their chances. When the big-money professionals do something a certain way, I figure there must be a reason for it.

Now I advocate keeping your chin up but following the fence with your eyes until it disappears under the front of your horse. This strategy makes perfect sense because your direct vision is simply more accurate than your peripheral vision. Watching the fence for a split second longer makes most riders 100 percent more accurate in their jumping because it allows them to stay back longer. I would much rather see a rider a little late in her release than a little premature. A rider who releases forward too early is loading extra weight on the horse's front end, making it harder for him to lift off the ground. If you make this mistake a second time, the horse may refuse to jump because he knows how uncomfortable the jump will be for him.

KEEP IT SIMPLE

Jumping can be a complicated matter; you can spend years studying and talking about the techniques, strategies, and philosophies of jumping. It can easily take a half-hour to walk the course before a horse show, even though it will take only sixty seconds to ride it. When you are sitting on the horse galloping toward the fence, you need to keep it simple. Riders who think too much get themselves into trouble. Clear your mind. Ride and react.

A great trainer once gave me excellent advice about jumping. "Point your horse to the jump and kick him," he said. That was it. His point was that—no matter how much you study and learn—when you get to the fence, you're either ready or you're not. If you've done your homework properly, your developed instincts will take over when you get to the jump. Once there, you don't have time to analyze things.

I like to use gymnastic-type lines in my jump lessons: lots of short, choppy combinations in succession, like two-strides, one-strides, no-strides. I do this because a good gymnastic line eliminates the analysis. It forces you to ride forward and jump, to "point your horse and kick him."

Don't make jumping harder than it needs to be. If you let your horse pick a spot, doesn't he usually find the right one? Sometimes you can screw your horse up more than you can help him. Let him go forward and find a spot, then you can adjust and cover it. A tighter spot (takeoff spot closer to the jump) requires a bit more patience with your release, waiting a split second later to commit your upper body to the forward

release. A bigger spot takes a little more strength and quickness, since the jump comes to you a bit sooner than the ideal moment in the stride. With experience, riders develop a "good eye," or the ability to consistently gauge takeoff spots and to make these subtle adjustments accordingly.

If you're finding a good takeoff spot, moving forward in balance, and not inhibiting your horse, then you've done all you can do. After that, it's a matter of talent—either the horse can jump or he can't. Not every horse can jump even two feet. I have a barn full of "gravitationally challenged" horses. Three feet is getting pretty darned tough for some, and three feet, six inches really separates the stars from the rest. A good natural rider can certainly help a horse extend his range. But an overworking, overthinking rider can severely *limit* a horse's range.

Like most sports, jumping is a craft, and the longer you're around and the more you learn, the better you will become. No doubt, some people have very little aptitude for riding, including some people who love it most, but that's the exception. If you have natural balance and good, sound natural aid skills, you can learn to be a fairly good jumper.

MENTAL EQUITATION IN A NUTSHELL: COMMUNICATION, SIMPLICITY, PATIENCE, AND COMMITMENT

In any field of endeavor, knowledge is power. This book is full of information about a system that works for all riding disciplines, but remember there's a difference between information and *knowledge*. Knowledge implies understanding, which is usually gained through experience. Properly *understood*, the theories behind mental equitation can enable you to ride, train, and show your horse effectively.

Mental equitation teaches you how to speak the language of horsemanship, using strong natural aids to ask for what you want and insisting that your horse do exactly what you ask. Many riders are sloppy with their natural aids, sending unintentional signals and making the horse interpret a dialect. Mental equitation makes it possible to ride with enough precision to say what you mean and mean what you say.

Some people go so far as to develop their own unique language for communicating with the horse. Why reinvent the wheel? You shouldn't have to make up a language if you're using a communication system based on classical horsemanship theory. Mental equitation elicits the desired response by taking advantage of the horse's natural instincts. No matter what you call it, if you're using such a system, you are communicating!

Mental equitation lets you pass up the tack store gimmicks that offer miracle cures and overnight results. Good, sound training comes from good, sound natural aids, and natural aids are not complicated! If someone makes a claim about a piece of tack and it doesn't make sense to you, beware. The best trainers know that every piece of tack has a place and a purpose and that each horse is different. Your job is to figure out what makes a given horse tick, and then apply the concepts or tack that will help him. Mental equitation keeps your training system as simple as possible, saving you a lot of time, money, energy, and worry.

As helpful as it is, mental equitation does not *instantly* change your riding or training. If your horse was once accustomed to a different system of aids, remember that it may seem to him that he has a new rider. Give him time to adjust. Understanding and implementing mental equitation is like developing any other skill: comprehending the concepts will probably come more quickly than your ability to apply them. The more you use mental equitation, the better you will become at using it, and the more pronounced the results will be.

Success seldom comes easily. If you want to be a top competitor, or a professional, you can't expect to ride once a week. Successful people in any field spend countless hours trying to get to the top. Inevitably, major league baseball players were the kids who spent four hours a day throwing a rubber ball against the side of the house. As one former major leaguer told me, if you spend enough time at something, you'll get pretty good at it. The key is to spend more time at it than anyone else. World champion riders and horses are the product of hard work, knowledge, experience, and desire. If you're committed to what you're doing, it will show.

Mental equitation gives you the tools to achieve excellence. The mental equitation concepts that make you a winner in the arena will make you a winner in every aspect of your life. Allow yourself the chance to do your best. Live with confidence in your own abilities. Never let anybody tell you that "you can't." People with a passion *can* succeed. As a rider, trainer, and coach, I'm betting on it!

With this win in 1993, Ohio State University became the first team ever to win three consecutive National Championships in Western division. Coaches Debbie and Ollie Griffith are on the ends. They have also won the 1996 and 1997 Championships, as, making them the only team to have won five times.

Index

A

above the bit, 79
active aids, 37
appearance, personal, 103-104
artificial aids, 35-36, 53-63
attitude, 103

B

backing, 29, 101-102
balance, 118-119, 125
behavior (horse), 2, 5-17, 81
behind the bit, 27
binocular vision, 58, 62
bitting rigs, 63
blind spot, 8-9
body balance (horse), 98
body language (horse), 11-12
bosal, 11, 33, 62
breeding, 32

C

canter, 28-30, 33, 39, 44, 51, 55, 76, 81-83, 93, 98, 115
center of balance, 23-28, 45
circle, 43-44, 69-71, 87, 91, 99-100
collection, 57, 65, 76, 78-79, 81,100, 112, 115-116, 122
color-blind, 9
communication 1-2, 35-36, 39, 78-79, 98, 102, 110, 127-128
competitive riders, 95
conformation, 20
correlation response, 14
course, 115
crop, 55-57
croup, 20-21, 24
curb bits, 57-58, 63
Pelham, 58

Kimberwicke, 58
Tom Thumb, 41, 58, 63
Western Grazing, 58
Half-spade, 58
curb chain, 58-59, 81
curb rein, 58, 81

D

dexterity, 8
direct rein, 40-44, 70-72
discipline, 1-2, 11, 16, 19-32, 45, 57, 65, 77, 96-98, 109-125
displacing leg, 37-38, 44, 72, 82, 84, 87-88, 90
dominant horse, 7
downward transitions, 14, 78, 84
draw reins, 58-63
dressage riders, 56, 118
dummy bump, 9
dynamic balance, 24-26

E

English technique, 85
English trot, 27
equitation classes, 96, 98
evasions of the bit, 79
executing a straight line, 100
executing the circle or turn, 100

F

fight or flight, 7
finishing a horse, 65
fixed aids, 59-61
flying change, 91, 121-122
follow-through, 85
footfall patterns, 26-29
forearm, 20-22
forehand assembly, 21
full-seat, 112
fundamentals, 65-73

G

gait, 26, 55-56, 76, 78, 81, 101
gallop, 8, 29, 33, 112, 115
going on the line, 66-69
gregarious nature, 6
ground poles, 110-112

H

hackamore, 11, 66
half-halt, 47, 85
half-seat, 112
halt, 113
head and neck, 20-24
head-setting devices, 80
hearing, 9-10
heredity, 32
high-headed horse, 61
hindquarters, 20, 68, 75, 78, 82, 89-90
horizontal engagement, 76
horse show, 95-96, 98, 102-107, 111, 113
horsemanship, 13, 26, 35, 96, 98, 111, 127
hunter, 10, 22, 42-43, 55-56, 66, 76-77, 98, 103,
    110, 112-115, 118

I

impulsion, 20, 37, 56, 65, 73, 75, 90, 115-118
inactive leg aid, 37-38
in front of the bit, 79-80
indirect rein, 40, 42-44
individual patterns, 105-106
inside leg aids, 36
inside-out, 81-83
instinctive behavior, 5
interdisciplinary, 1, 111-112
intuition, 11

J

jump course, 115-124
jumping, 109-125

L

lateral agility, 87-93
lateral aids, 87

lateral weight displacement, 50
lateral work, 101
lead change, 91, 100-101
leading rein, 40-41
learned instincts, 12-13
leg aids, 36-38
leg positions, 38-39
leg yielding, 90, 101
leverage devices, 57-63
longeing, 16, 63, 99
longitudinal agility, 13, 23-25, 65-66, 75-86
longitudinal balance, 22
low knees, 21

M

marble spurs, 54-55
mechanics of motion, 26
memory (horse), 2, 12
mental equitation system, 2, 75
mental preparation, 103
monocular vision, 7, 62

N

natural aids, 25, 35-51, 65-68, 81, 87, 95, 100, 122,
    127
natural instincts, 5, 127
neck rein, 11, 14-15, 40, 42-43, 57, 71, 81, 87,
    89-90
nervous riders, 11
nicker, 12

O

outside-in, 81-83

P

passive seat, 72
pecking order, 6-7
perfectionism, 195
physical preparation, 96-98
pivot, 9, 87, 89-90, 106
plan, 113-114, 122-124
practice, 2, 8, 16, 19, 54. 57, 63, 68-69, 85, 95-96,
    101-103, 112-116, 123

ABOUT THE AUTHOR

JIM ARRIGON is Director of Horsemanship at Miami University, in the Cincinnati suburb of Oxford, Ohio. He is also coach of the nationally ranked Miami University Equestrian Team. During the past ten years, he has coached a National Champion team, two Reserve National Champion teams, and two other teams into the top four rankings in the nation. He has coached fifteen National Champion and Reserve Champion riders in hunt seat equitation on the flat and over fences, and in Western horsemanship.

Arrigon is the first (and to date, only) person to win the American Quarter Horse Association Trophy for Intercollegiate National Champion Western Team as both a rider and coach, having competed as an open rider on the 1979 and 1980 National Champion teams for Miami University, and coaching the 1985 Murray State University (Kentucky) team. In 1980, he was the Reserve National Champion Intercollegiate High Point Western Rider.

He has served on the Intercollegiate Horse Show Association (IHSA) Board of Directors

for nearly a decade, and has served as its secretary since 1991. The IHSA is the sanctioning body for college equestrian sports.

Arrigon has published instructional articles in many major equestrian magazines, including *Chronicle of the Horse, Horse World USA, Quarter Horse Journal,* and *Western Horseman.*

With a Bachelor of Science from the University of Kentucky and a Masters in Equine Science from Murray State University, Arrigon has worked in breeding farm management in both the Thoroughbred and Quarter Horse industries. He also produces horse shows, including the prestigious "Tournament of Champions" collegiate shows and the 1993 Intercollegiate National Championships. He is now involved in developing an NCAA equestrian team as the newest NCAA sport.

Arrigon lives in Hamilton, Ohio, with his wife, Gwen, their two children Matthew and Hallie, and Jack Russell, Sadie. They operate Three Chimneys Farm on an historic 1835 estate.